Literary Strolls in Wiltshire & Somerset

Gordon Ottewell

Published by Sigma Leisure – an imprint of
Sigma Press, 1 South Oak Lane, Wilmslow, Cheshire SK9 6AR, England.

British Library Cataloguing in Publication Data
A CIP record for this book is available from the British Library.

ISBN: 1-85058-760-4

Typesetting and Design by: Sigma Press, Wilmslow, Cheshire.

Cover photograph: Inglesham Church, Wiltshire *(Gordon Ottewell)*

Maps and photographs: Gordon Ottewell with additional photography by Graham Tavener

Printed by: MFP Design and Print

Disclaimer: the information in this book is given in good faith and is believed to be correct at the time of publication. No responsibility is accepted by either the author or publisher for errors or omissions, or for any loss or injury howsoever caused. Only you can judge your own fitness, competence and experience.

Preface

It would be hard to find two neighbouring counties boasting a richer array of literary associations than Wiltshire and Somerset. This is hardly surprising, considering the exceptional scenic diversity to be found within their respective borders. Such a variety of landscapes – sweeps of downland, ancient forest remnants, lush river valleys and levels, noble hills and a superb stretch of coastline – have combined to inspire writers of every description over the centuries. Some of these writers were born and bred within the counties, others were drawn to settle here in later life; yet others, though mere visitors, bestowed valuable literary offerings to mark their brief association.

This book is intended to enable the reader to discover the delights of strolling, standing and staring at some of the sights that these men and women found inspirational. Like them, the reader is invited to linger and look, to savour and reflect, before moving on.

Turning to practicalities, the book is essentially a strollers' guide. It consists of 40 short circular walks, none longer than 4 miles, many with shorter alternatives. Each has a literary connection – be it poet, novelist, diarist, essayist, naturalist – while some have more than one association.

Wherever possible, the routes of the strolls follow public footpaths, bridleways and quiet country lanes. Busy roads are almost entirely avoided. As with all country walks, the weather and farming activities influence the state of the routes and allowance should be made for mud, growing crops, rampant late-summer growth of resilient weeds on seldom-used paths, and the presence of livestock (dog owners beware!). Incidentally, a walking stick may come in handy as a nettle-basher and deterrent to over-attentive cattle.

Not everyone will want to place undue emphasis on the literary aspect of the strolls. The choice is yours. Whatever your preference, the routes should provide hours of healthy enjoyment out-of-doors and on foot in two of the fairest counties in the land.

Gordon Ottewell

Acknowledgements

I am greatly indebted to a number of people who gave me their whole-hearted help and encouragement in the writing of this book.

Once again, Bill Cronshaw's expertise proved invaluable in transforming my rough and ready typescript into acceptable form.

Ken Watts, whose knowledge of his native Wiltshire is truly encyclopaedic, not only accompanied me on many of the strolls in his county but also provided me with a mass of detailed information.

Similarly, Richard Emeny gave freely of his time and knowledge of Somerset and shared some of my Exmoor and Quantock wanderings.

David Bromwich, Wilf Deckner and Philip Stoyle, of the Somerset Library Service, provided much useful information on the county, as did my friend Shirley Toulson.

Graham Tavener, a Wiltshireman by adoption, kindly provided several of the photographs of that county and also gave valuable help with the photography generally.

Closer to home, I was glad of the willing help provided by my friends Elizabeth Thomas, Alec Betterton, and Morag and Geoff Adlington in various aspects of my researches.

I must also acknowledge the friendly assistance given by librarians and tourist information officers in both counties.

Last, but by no means least, I thank Margaret my wife, for her patience and practical help.

In acknowledging these contributions, I wish to make it clear that any inaccuracies, oversights or other shortcomings the book may have are mine and mine alone.

Gordon Ottewell
Winchcombe, Gloucestershire

Contents

Somerset Strolls

Key to symbols used on sketchmaps

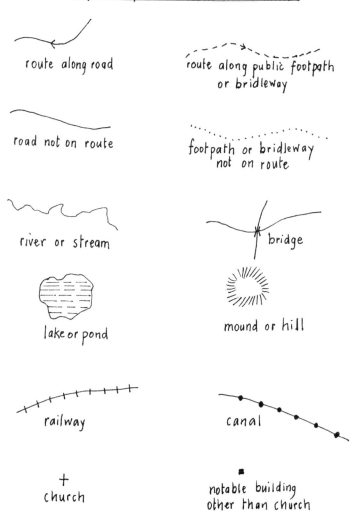

route along road

route along public footpath
or bridleway

road not on route

footpath or bridleway
not on route

river or stream

bridge

lake or pond

mound or hill

railway

canal

+
church

notable building
other than church

Introduction

Using the Book

For convenience, the strolls are arranged first according to county and then sub-divided into seven geographical areas, as follows:

Wiltshire

Swindon and South Cotswolds area	7 strolls
Chippenham and Devizes area	7 strolls
Salisbury and Warminster area	7 strolls

Somerset

Wells, Frome, Cheddar area	4 strolls
Yeovil and Somerton area	5 strolls
The Quantocks area	6 strolls
Exmoor area	4 strolls

The routes of the strolls are supplemented by the numbers of the relevant Ordnance Survey sheets, notes on parking, the nature of the terrain and suggested hostelries offering refreshment.

A simplified location map appears at the start of each section, showing main towns and roads as well as the precise locations, underlined, of the individual villages from which the strolls begin. Also provided are detailed sketch maps to accompany each stroll. These are intended not only to complement the route descriptions but also to provide additional information for those wishing to extend the strolls (see key to symbols).

Obtaining the recommended books

Many of the books referred to in the text as 'Recommended reading' are out of print and there is little prospect of them being re-issued, at least not in the immediate future. However, it is well worth enquiring at libraries for copies, as in the author's experience, librarians go to considerable lengths to track down requested titles.

Readers wishing to buy their own copies of out-of-print books are strongly advised to enquire at second-hand bookshops or through the equivalent web site such as www.bibliofind.com. Many of these offer a booksearch service for titles not currently in stock and, given time, will more often than not obtain books at reasonable prices, allowing for search and postage costs.

Wiltshire Strolls

Swindon and South Cotswolds Area

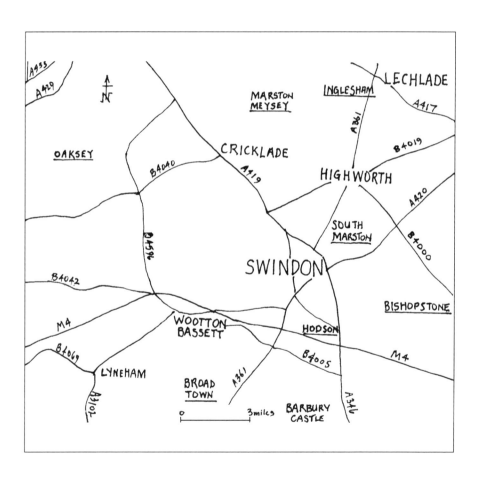

1. A Canal, a Craftsman and a Church
William Morris at Inglesham

Distance: 2½ miles

Location: Inglesham. The hamlet lies off the A361, one mile SW of Lechlade.

Park and Start: Lechlade. The stroll commences from the market place (limited car parking) in the centre of the town.

Maps: OS Landranger 163. OS Explorer 170. Grid ref. 214995

Terrain: A little pavement walking but chiefly along field paths, which may be muddy after rain. Level throughout.

Refreshments: Choice of inns and teashops in Lechlade

Route

1. From the market place, follow the A417 towards Cirencester. Cross the A361 (traffic lights) and continue to reach a lay-by in front of houses on the left. At the far end of the lay-by, cross a concrete stile to follow a signposted footpath.

2. Beyond a second stile, the path crosses fields by way of four stiled footbridges. After crossing these, continue over one more stile to reach a lane.

3. Turn left here, and left again in 20 metres along a private road (public footpath) leading to the Round House. Follow this over a cattle grid and as far as a 'private' sign. At this point, the path goes off to the left, following the River Coln on the last short stretch of its journey to meet the Thames.

4. Cross the footbridge. (The Round House, built at the confluence of the Thames and the now abandoned Thames-Severn Canal, can be glimpsed through the trees on the right).

5. From the bridge, the footpath to Inglesham strikes off across the field to reach a stiled footbridge. Beyond this, cross a second field. (The site of the medieval village lies to the left). Aim to the left of trees to reach a lane via a stile.

6. Turn right into Inglesham.

7. To return to Lechlade, retrace the outward route as far as the Thames

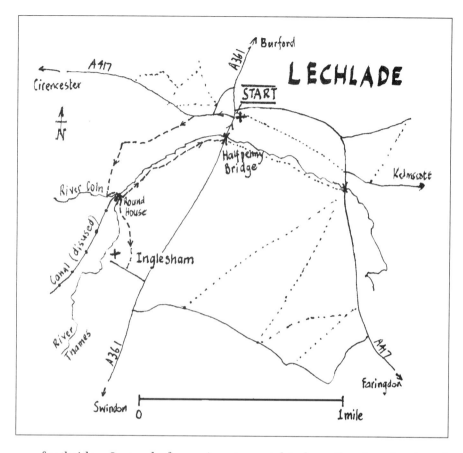

footbridge. Instead of crossing, turn right along the river bank and follow it all the way to the Halfpenny Bridge, carrying the A361 (the Swindon road) over the Thames.

8. Cross the bridge and walk up to the traffic lights. Turn right back to the start.

Literary Connections

The name Inglesham appears three times on Ordnance Survey maps on that north-east tip of Wiltshire that ends on the edge of the little Gloucestershire town of Lechlade. To the south, the huddled farms and cottages of Upper Inglesham flank the A361, while a mile or so to the north, between that bustling highway and the River Thames, lie the humps and hollows of the deserted medieval village of Inglesham.

Inglesham church

Alongside, and closer still to the river, with only a house and farm for company, and approachable by wheeled traffic only along a narrow lane, stands a church that was dear to the heart of that many-talented Victorian, William Morris. This is Inglesham, and the church of St John the Baptist is one of the few that has survived virtually unaltered since Tudor times. It is to Morris himself that we are indebted for this remarkable survival. For although the architect J.T. Micklethwaite carried out extensive repairs in 1888, Morris was involved throughout and as a result the worst excesses of Victorian restoration were entirely avoided.

Maintained now by the Churches Conservation Trust, the church deserves a leisurely visit. Not to be missed are wall paintings from the 13th and later centuries, ancient screens, pulpit and box pews and a late Saxon Virgin and Child in which the bodies are depicted in profile but the heads in full face.

Inglesham lies in the heart of 'William Morris country'. It was in 1871 that the artist, craftsman, poet and visionary came to live nearby at Kelmscott Manor. 'Though the country ... is not remarkable,' he wrote later, 'every turn and every byway set me a-longing to go afoot through the country, never stopping for a day.'

Eighty years earlier, Inglesham had been chosen as the point on the

Thames, alongside its confluence with a tributary, the Coln, at which the 29-mile canal linking that river with the Severn should be made. A lock and wharf were built, together with a three-storeyed roundhouse for the lock-keeper. The canal has long since been abandoned and both lock and wharf have disappeared. The roundhouse, hidden by trees, is now a private residence.

The canal was intended as a trade waterway and passenger traffic was actively discouraged, as the poet Shelley and friends discovered in 1815. Arriving from Lechlade after having rowed up the Thames from Windsor, they found to their dismay that they would have had to pay twenty pounds – the same sum as a fully laden barge – to navigate the canal to reach the Severn. Instead, the party terminated their travels at Lechlade, where Shelley was inspired to write a poem in praise of the churchyard.

Nearby Stroll

A Cotswold Character: Reginald Arkell at Marston Meysey (page 7).

2. A Cotswold Character

Reginald Arkell at Marston Meysey

Distance: 1 mile

Location: Marston Meysey. The village lies 2½ miles NE of Cricklade on an unclassified road linking the A419 at Cricklade with the A417 at Fairford.

Park and Start: In the village street, near the church, from which the stroll begins

Maps: OS Landranger 163. OS Explorer 169. Grid ref.128972

Terrain: Village street and short stretches of bridleway and footpath, both of which may be muddy after rain. Level throughout.

Refreshments: The Old Spotted Cow Inn

Route

1. Facing the Victorian church of St James, turn left along the village street. The Cotswold character of the village is immediately apparent: farmhouses, barns and cottages built with locally quarried limestone in traditional styles, many of 17th-century origin, though interspersed with recent buildings of variable quality. It is easy to understand how Marston Meysey has competed successfully for the best-kept village award, as can be seen from the emblem displayed in front of the converted school, now serving as a village hall.

2. Pass the garage, formerly a traditional Cotswold barn – a change from the ubiquitous conversion to luxury home.

3. The house on the right, immediately beyond the phone box, and now called 'Breakpools', was formerly known as 'Green Fingers', and was the home of the writer and poet Reginald Arkell and his actress wife Elizabeth. A fleeting glimpse can be had of the beautiful and extensive garden behind this old and graceful Cotswold house.

4. Retrace steps towards the start. On the right, just before drawing level with the church, is a bridleway signposted to Castle Eaton and Kempsford. A pleasant three-quarter mile diversion can be made from here as follows:-

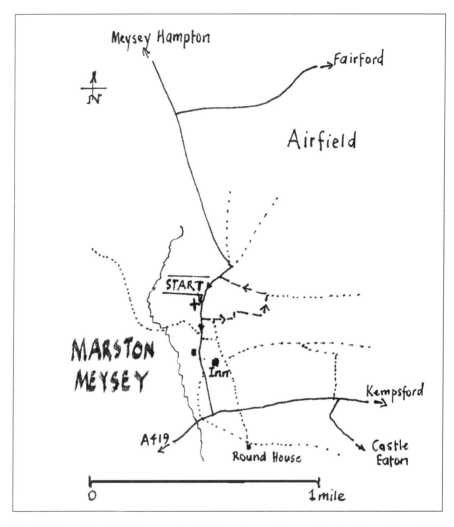

5. Follow the bridleway straight on, ignoring a side-track on the right. Continue between hedges to reach a wood on the left.

6. The bridleway turns to the left round the perimeter of the wood before swinging sharp right at its end towards the Gloucestershire hamlet of Dunfield.

7. Turn left along the footpath beside the wood, back to Marston Meysey, reaching the village street over a stile.

8. Turn left back to the start, through the northern end of the village, not seen previously. A good view of the fine Cotswold manor house, set back from the road, can be had from the churchyard.
Note: Canal enthusiasts will be aware that the line of the former Thames-Severn Canal can be traced to the south of Marston Meysey. Unfortunately, the canal round house, one of five built along the waterway round about 1790, has now been incorporated into a private house and together with a humpback bridge, can no longer be inspected at close quarters. (See map).

Marston Meysey: former 'Greenfingers'

Literary Connection

It was in the early 1930s, some time before the construction of the vast airbase that sprawls across its northern boundary, that the popular and versatile writer Reginald Arkell (1882-1959) and his actress wife Elizabeth, came to live at Marston Meysey. The son of a farmer, and from a family of noted brewers, Arkell was a Gloucestershire man, born at nearby Lechlade, and he often joked that if only he could divert the stream at the bottom of his garden to flow round the front of his house, he would still be living in his native county.

Reginald Arkell began his working life as a journalist but soon made his mark as a playwright. His first success, *Columbine*, was staged in both London and Chicago before the First World War. After war service, his theatrical career took off, with a series of revues, operettas and musicals bringing him fame and fortune. His native Cotswolds exerted their irresistible pull however, and once happily established at Marston Meysey, he embarked on another successful career – that of country novelist, together with books of whimsical humorous poetry, notably about gardens and gardeners, and with a study of Richard Jefferies and his countryside thrown in for good measure.

But it is for his story of Bert Pinnegar, an elderly gardener known as 'Old Herbaceous', that Reginald Arkell is perhaps best remembered today. First published in 1950, the novel was dramatised in 1979 by Alfred Shaugnessy and received its premiere at Salisbury before transferring to the Mayfair Theatre, London, for a highly acclaimed season.

'Old Herbaceous' has since been produced in the United States and Zimbabwe and a condensed version has appeared on television. More recently still, it has been recorded on video with Roger Hume starring as Bert Pinnegar and Roger Clissold directing.

Recommended reading:

Old Herbaceous, Reginald Arkell. 1950.

Richard Jefferies and his Countryside, Reginald Arkell. 1946.

Nearby stroll

A Canal, a Craftsman and a Church: William Morris at Inglesham (page 3).

3. A Diarist with a Difference
Elspeth Huxley at Oaksey

Distance: 2½ miles

Location: Oaksey. The village lies 2 miles east of the A429, 7 miles NE of Malmesbury.

Park and Start: On the village street, near the church, from which the stroll begins

Maps: OS Landranger 163. OS Explorer 168. Grid ref. 991936

Terrain: A mixture of pavement, minor road and fieldpath walking. The field paths can be muddy after rain. Virtually level throughout.

Refreshments: Wheatsheaf Inn

Route

1. Facing the church gate, turn left and walk the short distance to a crossroads. Turn left, passing a fine twin-gabled Cotswold-style house to reach a stile alongside the Wheatsheaf Inn, leading to a public footpath signposted to Kemble Wick.

2. The footpath follows a surfaced track almost as far as its junction with a lane. To continue along it, cross a stile on the left and keep to the hedge side.(After rain, it is advisable to walk along the lane itself as far as a sharp right-hand bend).

3. The footpath crosses a footbridge before reaching the lane at the bend by the entrance to the drive to Dean Farm.

4. Cross the stile at the bend (Kemble Wick signpost). Keep a hedge on the left and continue to cross a stile in a hedge. Still with a boundary on the left, continue to cross a footbridge with a stile at either end.

5. Cross two more stiles. Immediately beyond the second, at a meeting point of four hedges, turn sharp left (no waymark at the time of writing) to go through a gap and cross a field, aiming for the left-hand corner of a wood. (Dean Plantation).

6. On reaching this corner, follow the grassy track to the right as far a fence-stile straight ahead. Cross a field, aiming for a gateway in the opposite corner, with the buildings of Dean Farm ahead.

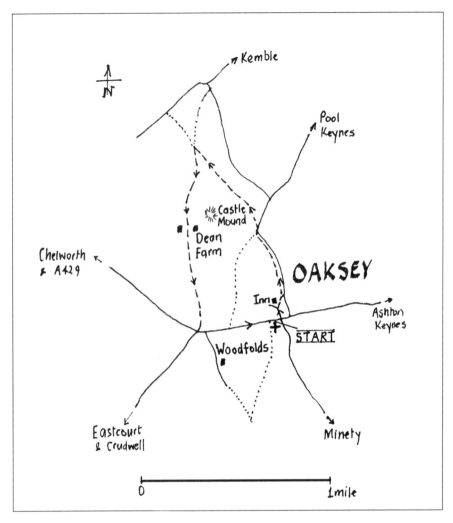

7. Go through the gateway and approach the farm, keeping a hedge on the left and a ditch on the right. The site of Norwood Castle (Norman motte and bailey), described by John Aubrey in the 17th century as 'a little citadel with a keepe hill, both moated round', lies to the left, with a water tower alongside.

8. Cross the farm drive via stiles. An excellent view can be had to the left of the 18th-century farmhouse. Beyond the second stile, cross a field, aiming for the far right-hand corner.

9. Cross another field. Go over a stile and a footbridge and follow the clearly defined track, reaching the western edge of Oaksey after a gentle climb. Go through a handgate leading to a lane and so to the village street.

10. Turn left along the street. To see 'Woodfolds', former home of Elspeth Huxley, turn right almost immediately along the Green (no through road). 'Woodfolds' stands back on the left beyond the other houses.

11. To return to the start, follow the street back to the church. Opposite the three storeyed Street Farm, notice the decorated door and window lintels of No 8 cottage, believed by Elspeth Huxley to have come from a long-lost manor house that stood behind the church.

Literary connection

From 1941 until her death, aged 89, in 1997, Oaksey was the home of Elspeth Huxley, author of over thirty books, ranging from biographies of Florence Nightingale and David Livingstone to an autobiographical trilogy set in Africa, where she spent much of her early life.

In 1976 however, she extended her range of subject matter even wider

'Woodfolds', Oaksey

with the publication of *Gallipot Eyes*, subtitled *A Wiltshire diary*, which as the latter suggests, is a personal record of life in this north Wiltshire village, compiled between April 1974 and March 1975.

Arranged in monthly sections, *Gallipot Eyes* is a delightfully idiosyncratic mixture of daily happenings, interspersed with intriguing snippets of local history. In her preface, the author stresses that the book is not intended as a village history, yet there is much absorbing history within its pages. Elspeth Huxley, the reader soon discovers, was a good listener, and her book is a valuable record of village life as experienced by older villagers, 'who can recall a past already as foreign to the young as the plains of Tartary'.

There is a generous spicing of humour, too, within the pages of this unique diary. We read, among other anecdotes, of the alarm caused by the arrival of a television camera team, of a rector who dismissed the Old Testament as a collection of fairy tales, and of a lady of the manor who served her maids with morning tea.

Like Elspeth Huxley herself, the old folks described with skill and affection in *Gallipot Eyes*, have passed on. Oaksey too is not the Oaksey of old, yet sufficient remains to enable the visitor to relate to the village so lovingly described in this engaging book.

The name of Oaksey is a familiar one in horse racing circles. Lord Oaksey, who still lives and farms locally, was a famous amateur jockey until injury compelled him to retire. He is now best known as a commentator and as author of a book on the celebrated racehorse Mill Reef.

Recommended reading

Gallipot Eyes, Elspeth Huxley, Weidenfeld and Nicholson, 1976. Republished by Picton Publishing, 1996.

4. Where Two Scholars Settled

Geoffrey Grigson and Nikolaus Pevsner at Broad Town

Distance: 3¼ miles (optional extension of an extra three-quarters of a mile, involving retracing steps)

Location: Broad Town. The village lies off the A4361, 5 miles SW of Wroughton.

Park and Start: Clyffe Pypard, a village 1½ miles SW of Broad Town and reached from the A4361 either via Broad Hinton or Winterbourne Bassett. Park on the left-hand verge of the loop lane on the west of the village centre (see map).

Maps: OS Landranger 173. OS Explorer 157. Grid ref. 069765

Terrain: Minor roads and field paths, which may be muddy after rain. Gentle gradients only.

Refreshments: Goddard Arms, Clyffe Pypard

Route

1. From the suggested parking place, walk down the lane. Turn right at the bottom and left at the next junction. Pass the Goddard Arms on the right and continue towards the church along a drive on the right. The churchyard gates, erected in the 1960s, incorporate the initials of Lola and Nikolaus Pevsner.

2. On the left of the path before it leaves the churchyard can be seen the slate gravestone of the Pevsners.

3. Continue, passing a lake on the left, to enter a field. Go straight across and leave over a stile. Cross another field to go over a second stile followed by a footbridge. Now keep to the left-hand edge of a field. The path eventually becomes a track.

4. A white horse, carved on the hillside chalk, and dating from 1863, now comes into view ahead. Cross a stile by a gate and continue to a crossways.

5. Go straight over along Pye Lane into Broad Town. The house on the left at the crossroads, Broad Town Farmhouse, was the home of the

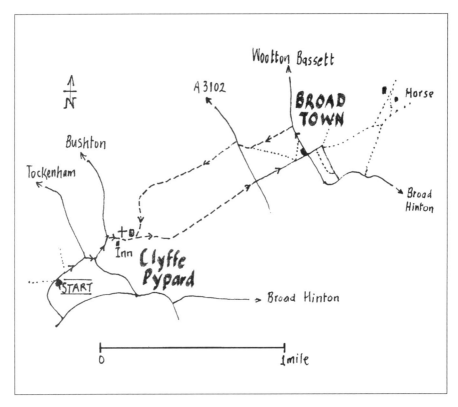

author and critic Geoffrey Grigson and his wife Jane, the cookery
writer. The main chimney bears the inscription: RS 1668.

Optional extension to the stroll

For a closer view of the white horse and a glimpse of Nikolaus Pevsner's
cottage, which involves retracing steps, continue along Chapel Lane,
opposite. The cottage comes into view behind trees on the right of the
track in less than half a mile.

6. To resume the stroll from the crossroads, and facing Chapel Lane,
   turn left along the road to reach a footpath on the left by a phone box.
   The path follows the left-hand field boundary at first. When this
   swings sharply away to the left, the path continues straight on across
   a field to reach a lane. (Note: This path was obliterated by crops at
   the time of writing, which necessitated retracing steps along Pye
   Lane and turning right at the crossways to join the intended route).

The White Horse and Pevsner's cottage

7. The route now follows a concrete farm track (yellow waymark on fence) on the left, a short distance from the point at which the fieldpath joins the lane. Beyond barns, continue through a gateway and straight on, with a hedge on the left.

8. Climb a stile and continue to cross another, by a giant ash tree. Now cross a field diagonally left to reach and follow a hedgerow as far as a gap.

9. With a hedge on the right, cross one more field to join the outward route near the lake. Retrace steps to the start.

Literary Connections

Although modest in size, the village of Broad Town was for several years the home of two men whose writings, though widely different, placed them in the forefront of the authorities on the English countryside.

Geoffrey Grigson (1905-1985) was a Cornishman, the seventh son of a vicar. In later life, following a varied career encompassing teaching, journalism, publishing and radio producing, he emerged as a respected if controversial critic, poet and author of numerous books on the countryside. His breadth of knowledge was phenomenal; as an obituarist wrote: "He could put a name to each and every flower, bird or insect he saw. It was a duty and an honour for him to be able to do so, since it displayed a proper respect for the varied naturalness of all living things".

Grigson came to live in Wiltshire in 1939, purchasing a semi-derelict cottage at Little Town. Seven years later, on moving to what was to be his last home, Broad Town Farmhouse, he offered the cottage to Nikolaus Pevsner (1902-1983), the German-born scholar, best known for his editorship of the celebrated *Buildings of England* series of county architectural guides. Like Grigson, Pevsner grew to love Wiltshire, and especially this somewhat remote corner of the county, and it seems appropriate that a refugee from Nazi Germany should be buried in a quiet churchyard in the county in which his scholarship is held in such high regard.

Recommended Reading

The Wiltshire Book, Geoffrey Grigson, 1957.

The Shell Country Book, Geoffrey Grigson, 1962.

The Shell Country Alphabet, Geoffrey Grigson, 1976.

The Buildings of England: Wiltshire, Nikolaus Pevsner, Penguin, 1963. (since revised)

Nearby Strolls

The Naturalist at Home: Richard Jefferies at Hodson (page 19)

The Hammerman Poet: Alfred Williams at Barbury Castle (page 23)

5. The Naturalist at Home
Richard Jefferies at Hodson

Distance: 1¾ miles

Location: Hodson. The hamlet lies off the B4005 between Wroughton and Chiseldon.

Park and Start: The lay-by opposite the Calley Arms at the southern approach to Hodson

Maps: OS Landranger 173. OS Explorer 169. Grid ref. 175863

Terrain: One short stretch of minor road, then field and woodland paths. Some rough going after summer growth. Gentle gradients.

Refreshments: Calley Arms, Hodson. Sun Inn, Coate.

Route

1. From the lay-by, walk into Hodson. On the left, just beyond the hollow known as Hodson Bottom, stands the thatched cottage, home of Haylock, the keeper featured in Richard Jefferies' book *The Gamekeeper at Home*, published in 1878.

Keeper's Cottage, Hodson

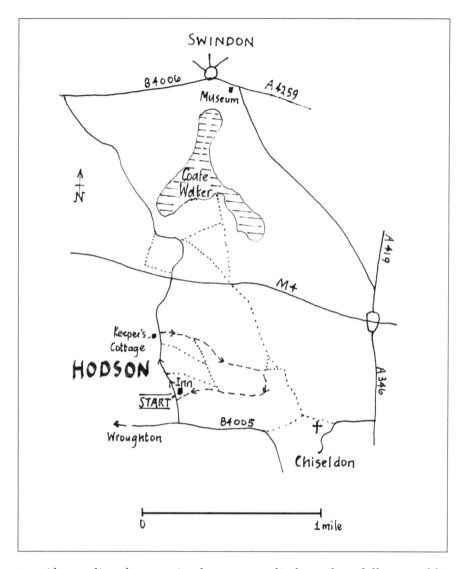

2. Almost directly opposite the cottage, climb a stile to follow a public
    footpath to the left, which climbs into woodland.

3. At the top of the slope, ignore a stile on the right. Instead, keep on to
    cross another stile, beyond which the path skirts a field edge.
    Liddington Hill, beloved by Jefferies, with its prominent tree clump,
    now comes into view ahead.

4. Ignore another stile on the right and continue to cross yet another straight ahead, bearing a yellow waymark. The path now meanders along a bank before eventually descending to join the waymarked Millennium Trail.

5. Turn right along the Trail. Cross a stile by a gate and descend into a hollow, known as Hodson Valley.

6. Turn right in this hollow, as indicated by the yellow waymark. There is a hedge on the right at first, then woodland. Cross a stile. About 100 metres beyond this stile, there is a waymark post by the woodland edge.

7. Turn left here across a field. When the path forks, keep to the left, climbing between bushes with a stream on the right. Cross a stile and follow the footpath up to meet the road alongside the Calley Arms.

Coate Water and the Richard Jefferies Museum

As the map shows, these two features are a short distance to the north of Hodson. Much of Coate Water is now a country park, although the SW corner is a bird sanctuary. There are several footpaths around the Water. The Jefferies museum, based in the author's former home, is open to visitors on the 1st and 3rd Sundays, May to September, 2 - 5 p.m.

Literary Connection

No Wiltshireman is more closely identified with the countryside of his boyhood than Richard Jefferies. Sadly, much of that countryside, of which he wrote so lovingly, is now transformed out of all recognition by the relentless spread of Swindon. Even so, as this stroll reveals, there remain a few quiet corners close to his former home of Coate Farm, which retain a semblance of their rural charm, and which can still delight the reader of Jefferies' writing.

Born in 1848, Richard Jefferies showed no inclination to follow his father into farming. Instead, he sought from his earliest years to indulge in his passion for nature and the open countryside and as a youth became known to the locals as "Loony Dick, poking about in the hedges". In fact, this utter absorption in his rural surroundings in all their facets was to provide him with sufficient subject matter to fill the many books and articles he wrote in his short life – he died at 38 – and to place him in the forefront of writers on the English countryside.

Visitors to the Jefferies museum, and in particular those who have read *Bevis*, will be well aware of the significance Coate Water played in the author's early life. Yet comparatively few seek out the tiny hamlet of Hodson, the setting for Jefferies' memorable *The Gamekeeper at Home*. Here, at Hodson Bottom, Keeper Haylock's cottage still stands, snug beneath its thatch, and it was here, years later, that Jefferies' biographer, Edward Thomas, and his sweetheart Helen, are supposed to have spent their secret 'honeymoon', described with such tenderness by Helen in her autobiographical *As it Was*, written after Thomas's death in the Great War.

Having seen the birthplace, Coate Water and Hodson, admirers of Jefferies may well wish to extend their explorations a few miles southwards to Barbury Castle and to Burderop Down, the hilltop over which runs an ancient track branching from the Ridgeway. Here, Jefferies communed with nature with the intensity that was in time translated into his *The Story of my Heart* and it is here that a sarsen stone stands in his memory, inscribed with words from that book:

"It is Eternity now. I am in the midst of it. It is about me in the sunshine."

Recommended Reading

The Gamekeeper at Home, Richard Jefferies, Numerous editions.

Bevis. The Story of a Boy, Richard Jefferies, Numerous editions.

Richard Jefferies, Edward Thomas, Faber, 1978.

As it Was, Helen Thomas, Heinemann, Several editions.

Note: Richard Jefferies also features in a stroll in the Somerset section. See The Naturalist's Summer (page 162)

Nearby Strolls

The Ridgeway Rambler: H.W. Timperley at Bishopstone (page 28).

The Hammerman Poet: Alfred Williams at Barbury Castle (page 23).

6. The Hammerman Poet

Alfred Williams at Barbury Castle

Distance: 2½ miles

Location: Barbury Castle Country Park. The Park, which is well signposted, lies 2 miles south of the B4005 at Chiseldon.

Park and Start: The country park car park. (Toilet facilities available)

Maps: OS Landranger 173. OS Explorer 169. Grid ref. 157762

Terrain: Minor roads, tracks and footpaths. Steepish gradients. Sturdy footwear recommended.

Refreshments: Available at warden's house at east end of park

Route

1. Leaving the car park, follow the approach road downhill. To see the Jefferies-Williams memorial stone overlooking Burderop Down, turn right for a short diversion over a stile alongside a metal gate in about 250 metres.

2. Back on the park approach road, continue for about half a mile to reach a track on the left, signposted 'Ridgeway Route for vehicles'. This is the original line of the Ridgeway. Follow it for about a mile to reach a road.

3. Turn left and left again in 50 metres to follow the Ridgeway into the country park.

4. On attaining the top of the slope, walkers wishing to take the direct route back to the start should continue straight on over the earthwork. However, those wishing to enjoy the views to the south and east should keep to the right and follow the ramparts round to regain the main path near a metal gate.

5. Go through the gate and keep the boundary on the right back to the start.

Alfred Williams at Barbury Castle and South Marston

Like his fellow Wiltshireman, Richard Jefferies, Alfred Williams was especially drawn to the Iron-Age hillfort of Barbury Castle and it is

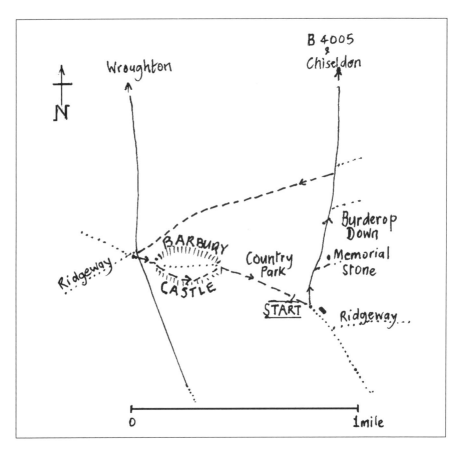

appropriate that the sarsen stone erected nearby in 1939 commemorates both men. Those wishing to visit Williams' home village of South Marston, reached off the A420 and approximately 10 miles to the north, may find the accompanying sketch-map useful. It shows the four houses in which he lived at various stages in his life (each bears a plaque) and also the church. Alfred's grave is to the left of the churchyard path beneath an overhanging larch bough.

Literary Connection

It would be hard to find a more moving story of one man's struggle against adversity than that of Alfred Williams. Born and bred in the village of South Marston, Williams (1877-1930) was one of eight surviving children, brought up in grinding poverty by his hard-working, intelligent

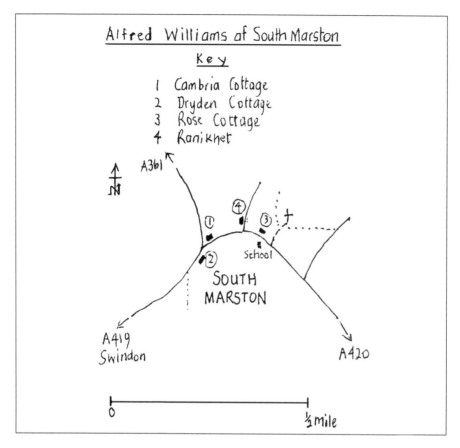

Alfred Williams of South Marston

Key

1 Cambria Cottage
2 Dryden Cottage
3 Rose Cottage
4 Ranikhet

A361

South Marston

A419
Swindon

A420

School

N

0 ——————————————— ½ mile

mother after his drunken father had walked out leaving extensive unpaid debts.

Alfred's full-time education ended at the age of eight when he began part-time work on a nearby farm. Leaving school finally at eleven, he toiled as a farm labourer for the next four years before joining his older brothers at the Great Western Railway works, walking the four miles there and back.

Promotion from rivet hotter to furnace boy and eventually to chargeman drop-stamper followed. Although he was eventually offered promotion to foreman, he declined, not wishing to be placed in a position of seniority over his workmates.

Sadly, these workmates, baffled by Alfred's studious nature – at 20 he had begun studying English literature, followed by Latin and Greek –

Alfred Williams' memorial, Burderop Down

began to taunt him. Undaunted, he embarked on a four-year course in English literature at Ruskin Hall, Oxford, rising early to read before walking to work and resuming his studies after returning in the evening.

In 1903, Williams married Mary Peck, whom he had known since she came to live in South Marston several years before. She was to be a loyal and patient wife and although the marriage proved childless, the couple found deep satisfaction in their country walks, which were later to inspire Alfred's poetry and books on Wiltshire and the Thames valley.

Between 1904 and 1914, when on doctor's orders he finally left the railway works, Williams managed, by sheer determination, to establish himself as both poet and author. *Songs in Wiltshire, Poems in Wiltshire* and *A Wiltshire Village*, although praised by the critics, brought their author meagre reward, despite his own efforts as a travelling salesman. In the meantime, he was working on *Life in a Railway Factory*, which was to be published after his departure from the GWR works, and which caused a considerable stir with its bold, provocative exposure of a hard and health-endangering life.

Now 37, and without a regular wage, Williams faced poverty. Helped by Mary, he tried to supplement the royalties from his books with market gardening, devoting what time remained to cycling to distant villages collecting folk songs. In 1916, despite his poor health, he enlisted in the army and was sent to India, which he came to love – so much so that on his return to civilian life he taught himself Sanskrit and wrote a book of Sanskrit tales. And as if that was not enough, he decided to build himself a house, using materials from a derelict cottage which he and Mary dismantled and transported to their chosen site by wheelbarrow. Named Ranakhet, after his Indian station, Alfred Williams lived there for the remainder of his life, scratching a living from his writings and market gardening. He died from exhaustion after cycling to visit Mary in hospital, who was herself dying of cancer. He was 53.

Recommended Reading

In a Wiltshire Village, Alfred Williams, Sutton 1981.

Round About Middle Thames, Alfred Williams, Sutton 1982.

Alfred Williams, His Life and Work, Leonard Clark, David and Charles, 1960.

Nearby Strolls

Where Two Scholars Settled: Geoffrey Grigson and Nikolaus Pevsner at Broad Town (page 15)

The Naturalist at Home: Richard Jefferies at Hodson (page 19)

7. The Ridgeway Rambler

H.W. Timperley at Bishopstone

Distance: 3 miles

Location: Bishopstone. The village stands on the unclassified Wanborough-Ashbury road, approximately midway between the B4192 at Liddington and the B4000/B4507 junction at Ashbury.

Park and Start: In the vicinity of the former millpond in the centre of the village

Maps: OS Landranger 174. OS Explorer 170. Grid ref. 246837

Terrain: A steady climb and descent along footpaths and bridleways, which may be muddy after rain. Followed by an easy village walkabout.

Refreshments: The True Heart and Royal Oak Inns

Route

1. From the pond, and the three storeyed former mill opposite, walk along the village street (part of the Icknield Way) eastwards towards Ashbury, passing the school and the village hall.

2. Turn right into Nell Hill (Russley Downs signpost). Spring Cottage, the white thatched former home of H.W. Timperley, lies along a narrow unmarked path immediately beyond the junction. In a short distance, follow the signposted footpath to the right along a lane. Beyond a house and garage, old watercress beds come into view below to the right, while strip lynchets can be seen on the steep bank above on the left.

3. Go through a kissing gate and cross a field to pass over a stile and enter a wide valley.

4. Do not cross the stile ahead on the right. Instead, continue up the valley, with high banks on either side, to pass through a gate. Beyond, a clear track climbs gently to reach the Ridgeway long-distance path.

5. Turn right. In about a third of a mile, and soon after passing a track on the left, turn right along a marked permissive path immediately before, and at first parallel to, a wide gated track.

6. Beyond a stile, this path veers to the right to descend by the terraces of an ancient field system to the stile referred to on the outward route.

7. From this stile, bear left. Go through a kissing gate and follow a bridleway (badly rutted and muddy after rain) back to Bishopstone.

8. On reaching the road, turn right for the direct route back to the start. Otherwise, turn left and immediately right along a no-through-road (West End Lane). At a junction, keep to the right along Church Lane. St Mary's church is reached along a drive to the right.

9. To complete the walk, retrace steps along the drive and turn right down an inviting grassy path to the right of the church car park. Cross a footbridge and keep to the right. When the path forks, go to the left and climb the bank to pass the Royal Oak Inn and reach the village street almost opposite the pond.

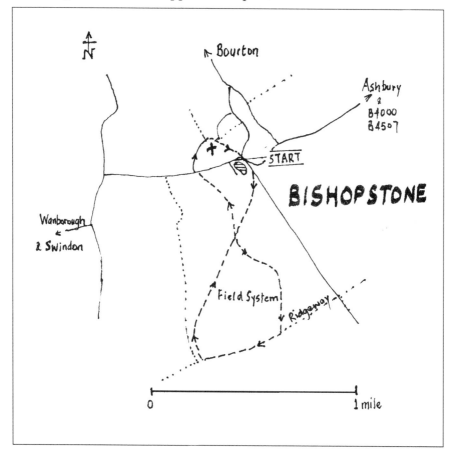

Literary connection

H.W. Timperley (1890-1961) was a native of Shropshire who discovered the delights of Wiltshire downland when training with the Territorial Army on Salisbury Plain. First and foremost a naturalist, he included three chapters on Wiltshire in his first book, *English Scenes and Birds (1929)*, which contained a highly appreciative introduction by H.J. Massingham. *A Cotswold Book* (1931) followed and this in turn was followed by *Ridge Way Country* (1935), in which the author evoked the subtle appeal of this ancient landscape in the spirit of those two native Wiltshiremen, Richard Jefferies and Alfred Williams, "whose footsteps I follow reverently".

Such was the impression that the village of Bishopstone and its downs made on Timperley that he devoted the first two chapters of *Ridge Way Country* to delicately descriptive essays on their irresistible appeal. "The village", he wrote, "snuggles into the Downs as if it had grown there rather than been built....Bishopstone gives me the clearest impression that it owes nothing to the valley and all to the Downs."

In common with other writers before and since, Timperley's curiosity was aroused by the ancient cultivation terraces or strip lynchets, that form such a distinctive feature of the coombe in which Bishopstone lies.

Spring Cottage, Bishopstone

Like Massingham, he was of the opinion that they originated from Saxon times, believing them to have been carved out by ploughing, which caused the soil to drift downwards and thus forming a kind of step between each ploughed strip.

At the time Timperley was writing, the watercress beds at the foot of the coombe were still being cultivated along the stream issuing from the spring line and flowing into the village to feed the millpond, though it is unclear whether or not the mill itself was still working.

What is certain is that Bishopstone had not yet been subjected to the use of the intrusive building styles and materials now in evidence here as elsewhere, retaining its "harmony of chalk walls and thatch for every change of light to touch with beauty and keep the village for the Downs".

In 1949, Timperley fulfilled a long-cherished ambition by coming to live in Spring Cottage at Bishopstone and, while resident there, wrote *The Vale of Pewsey* (1954). Later he collaborated with his wife, Edith Brill, in writing *Ancient Trackways of Wessex*, which was published after his death.

Recommended reading

Ridge Way Country. H.W. Timperley. Dent 1935.

English Downland. H.J. Massingham. Batsford 1936.

The Icknield Way. Edward Thomas. Constable 1913.

Exploring Historic Wiltshire (Vol. 1). Ken Watts. Ex Libris 1997.

The Oldest Road: The Ridgeway. J.R.L. Anderson. Whittet 1987.

Ancient Trackways of Wessex. Timperley and Brill. Phoenix House 1965.

Nearby Strolls

The Naturalist at Home: Richard Jefferies at Hodson (page 19)

The Hammerman Poet: Alfred Williams at Barbury Castle (page 23)

Chippenham and Devizes Area

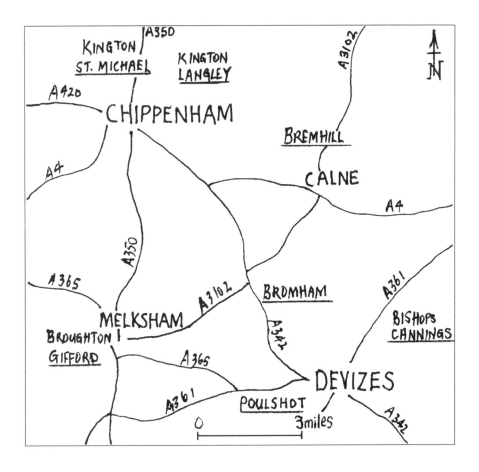

8. One Village – Two Historians

John Aubrey and John Britton at Kington St Michael

Distance: 2 miles (Route A). Short option of three-quarters of a mile (Route B)

Location: Kington St Michael. The village stands west of the A350, 2½ miles NW of Chippenham.

Maps: OS Landranger 173. OS Explorer 156. Grid ref. 905772

Terrain: A mixture of pavement and field path walking. The paths may be muddy after rain. Gentle gradients only.

Refreshments: The Jolly Huntsman Inn

Route A

Park and Start: At the approach to the church, at the south end of the village

1. On the village street, notice a plaque to John Britton, local historian, on the gable of the former village hall and a commemorative stone on the wall overlooking the pavement.

2. Turn left and walk up the village street. Pass the Jolly Huntsman Inn and Isaac Lyte's six-gabled almshouses (dated 1675). The plaque states that he was an Alderman of London. Note the coat of arms.

3. Continue along the street as far as a signpost to Easton Piercy on the left. Follow this road as far as a footpath sign on the right. Priory Farm can be seen ahead.

4. The path follows the left-hand edge of a football field before crossing a stone bridge and climbing through the Nymph Hay, a Woodland Trust plantation, dating from 1997.

5. Pass through a gate to reach a road and walk along the drive, passing between an impressive stone lion and the old Priory building.

6. Continue through a gateway and follow a grassy track towards woodland. Just before the track enters the wood, go through a metal gate on the left and along the wood side.

7. Cross two stiles and turn left to reach a road. On the right are fine buildings of Lower Easton Piercy farm.

8. Turn left and climb the road as far as a sharp left-hand bend.

9. Follow the waymarked footpath straight ahead, keeping a hedge on the right. At its end, continue straight on over a field to reach a hedged path through as gap.

10. Continue by crossing a stile. Kington St Michael church comes into view ahead. Keep a hedge on the right to a stile by a gate.

11. Cross straight over the next field to another stile by a gate. In the next field, aim for a stile in a hedge to the right of a clump of trees.

12. In the next field, keep the same line to a hedge corner. Keep a hedge on the right to reach a concrete farm road through a gate.

13. Follow this road round to the right, then left through the farmyard to reach and follow a lane back to the church and the start.

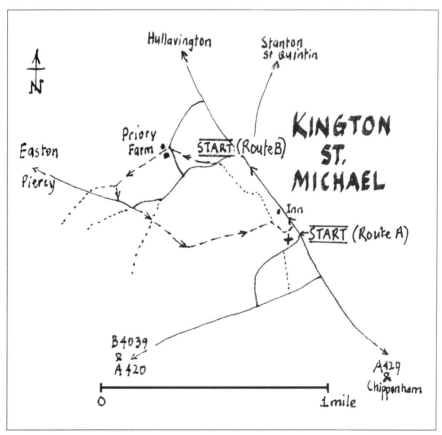

Route B

(Possibly combine with a stroll from the church along the village street).

Park and Start: At the north end of the village street at its junction with Grove Lane (Easton Piercy signpost. Grid ref. 900778)

Route

1. Walk along Grove Lane as far as a footpath sign on the right. Priory Farm can be seen ahead.
2. Follow the left-hand edge of the playing field down to a bridge. Cross and climb through Nymph Hay to reach a road.
3. Walk along the drive to see the Priory building to the left of a stone lion.
4. Retrace to the lane, turn right and follow it back to the start.

Literary Connections

Kington St Michael can boast that rare distinction of having produced two of Wiltshire's most eminent historians. The first of these, John Aubrey, ranks without doubt as one of the county's most celebrated sons. He was born at Lower Easton Place, Easton Piercy (long since destroyed) in 1626 and after receiving a basic education locally and in Dorset, went on to Oxford before entering the Middle Temple.

History was Aubrey's passion from early boyhood. Although he enjoyed social life and the thrill of the chase, his curiosity about the past led him to examine and record, among other things, the megalithic remains at Avebury. Inheriting his father's estate in his mid-thirties, Aubrey suffered a series of setbacks involving costly lawsuits and matrimonial difficulties, and was eventually ruined. However, this did not prevent him from embarking on a series of ambitious literary projects, including *The Natural History of Wiltshire, Topographical Collections, Miscellanies* (the only work published during his lifetime) and the book on which his national reputation rests, *Brief Lives Of Contemporaries*, which did not appear in print until 1898.

In one of Aubrey's papers appears a delightful description of the nuns from the priory at Kington (now Priory Farm), as described by an old villager, who saw them 'come forth into the Nymph Hay with their wheels to spin, and with their sewing work'.

Kington St Michael's second notable historian was John Britton (1771-1857), who is commemorated alongside Aubrey in a Victorian stained glass window in the church, as well as on a stone and plaque on

Kington St Michael church

the former village hall, said to stand on the site of his birthplace. The son of a village tradesman, Britton began his working life on a farm before the chance purchased of a bundle of books awakened a love of learning and prompted him to travel to London, where he became a winemerchant's apprentice.

Despite illness and limited means, Britton persevered with his studies and in time began to produce a series of books, beginning with *The Beauties of Wiltshire*, which was published in two volumes in 1801, and was followed by the 25-volume *Beauties of England and Wales*, which took over 20 years to complete. Works on archaeology and architecture followed and although Britton spent the rest of his long life in London and was buried there, many of his books, papers and drawings remain in Wiltshire, in the care of the county's archaeological society, of which he was a founder member.

Recommended Reading

A Literary Pilgrim in England, Edward Thomas, Various editions.

Wiltshire Portraits, Kenneth G. Ponting, Moonraker Press. 1975.

Nearby Strolls

In the Diarist's Footsteps: Francis Kilvert at Kington Langley (page 37)

The Parson Poet: William Bowles at Bremhill (page 41)

9. In the Diarist's Footsteps
Francis Kilvert around Kington Langley

Distance: 1½ miles

Location: Kington Langley. The village lies between the A350 and the B4069, 2½ miles north of Chippenham.

Park and Start: Near St Peter's church, at the junction of Plough Lane and Church Lane. Note: Limited parking only in the village. Patrons of the Hit or Miss Inn may make use of the car park.

Maps: OS Landranger 173. OS Explorer 156. Grid ref. 923769

Terrain: A mixture of road, grassy verge and field path walking. The paths can be muddy after rain. Gentle gradients only.

Refreshments: Hit or Miss Inn, Church Lane

Note of interest: Kilvert's church and school, Langley Burrell: Unfortunately, both these buildings, which figure frequently in Kilvert's diaries, stand on the busy B4069. However, the most interesting church (Grid ref. 928758) has a good car park. The former school (Grid ref. 928754) built in 1844 and Victorian Gothic, can be glimpsed in passing, a quarter of a mile to the south. Further south still, and standing back from the B4069 near its junction with the unclassified road to East Tytherton, is Kilvert's Parsonage, now a private house (Grid ref. 930749).

Route

1. Walk along Plough Lane as far as a public footpath signposted to Jacksom's Lane on the left.

2. The footpath is along a surfaced road at first. Beyond buildings, it continues as a path to reach a stile.

3. Beyond the stile, veer to the right down a field to cross a double stile. Continue over another field towards a cottage.

4. Cross a stile by a gate to the right of the cottage to reach Morrell's Lane, a wide grassy track, much frequented by Francis Kilvert and later, by Robin Tanner.

5. Turn right through a traffic barrier and climb the lane.

6. At the junction with Plough Lane, turn left to see Old Chapel Field, formerly the Tanners' home, standing on the right round the bend.

7. Retrace to pass the Morrell's Lane junction.

8. In about 20 metres, by a power pole, is the Poet's Gate. There is no record of the identity of the poet the original gate commemorated.

9. Continue back along Plough Lane to the start.

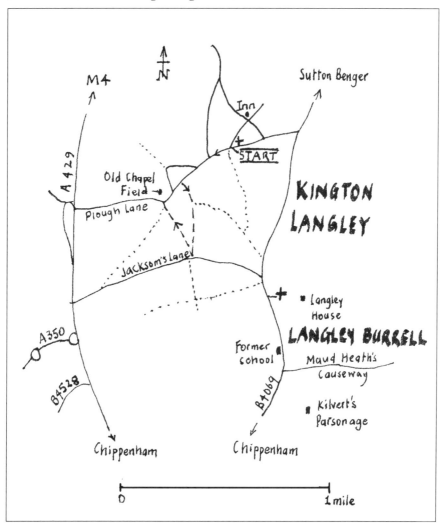

Literary Connections

Although he died in 1879, at the early age of thirty-eight, it was not until the publication in 1938 of selections from his diaries that the Rev. Francis Kilvert took his rightful place in the world of rural literature.

Born in 1840 at Hardenhuish Rectory, near Chippenham, the second child of the Rector, the Rev. Robert Kilvert, Francis received a private education before entering Wadham College, Oxford. Following his father into the church, he served as Robert's curate at Langley Burrell in 1863-4 and again, following a curacy at Clyro in Wales, from 1872 until 1876.

The diaries, closely written and filling no less than 22 notebooks, give a unique picture of late Victorian rural life, as seen through the eyes of a

Old Chapel Field, Kington Langley

sensitive, observant and articulate young cleric. They contain much social history, countless fresh and original impressions of the countryside, a flavouring of humour, and many memorable entries concerning the diarist's amorous hopes and fancies, in particular his ill-fated courtship of Ettie Meredith Brown, daughter of a wealthy local clergyman, who lived at Nonsuch House, Westbrook, which features in the stroll from Bromham (page 45).

Kilvert was a great walker and many of his diary entries give sufficient detail to enable the reader to locate the exact places described. One such entry, penned in March 1876, concerns Morrell Lane, Kington Langley, along which the diarist had walked with his beloved Ettie:

"I went on past the head of the steep green lane to the site of the old Chapel and burying place where my great-grandfather was laid to rest ... I lingered some time leaning over my favourite gate, the Poet's Gate, and looking at the lovely view."

Some sixty years later, the old Chapel field was bought by the artist and teacher Robin Tanner and his wife Heather. They built their Arts and Crafts-style house on the site and, determined to perpetuate the memory of Francis Kilvert, replaced the derelict Poet's Gate and dedicated the meadow it overlooked to the diarist.

Later, Robin and Heather Tanner were to add their own share of literary connections to Kington Langley through such beautifully produced books as *Wiltshire Village*, *Woodland Plants* and Robin's autobiography, *Double Harness*.

Recommended Reading

Kilvert's Diaries, Francis Kilvert, Jonathan Cape (several editions).

Francis Kilvert, David Lockwood, Seren, 1990.

Double Harness, Robin Tanner, Impact Books, 1987.

Nearby Strolls

One Village – Two Historians: John Aubrey and John Britton at Kington St Michael (page 33)

10. The Parson Poet

William Bowles at Bremhill

Distance: 2½ miles

Location: Bremhill. The village lies 1½ miles NW of Calne.

Park and Start: By the church

Maps: OS Landranger 173. OS Explorer 156. Grid ref. 980730

Terrain: Mostly over field paths, which can be muddy after rain. Gentle gradients only.

Refreshments: Dumb Post Inn

Route:

1. Go through the churchyard and leave through a metal gate at the far (west) end. A clear path leads along the field edge with sweeping views to the left.

2. Cross a stile and keep a boundary on the right. Cross another stile by a white gate to reach and follow a drive leading to a road.

3. Take the road signposted to Studley alongside the Dumb Post Inn. The road soon dips. Continue as far as a stile at a footpath sign on the right immediately before a house (Foxways).

4. Cross a field with woodland on the left and go over a double stile by a gate. Now cross a field to a stile to the right of a gate.

5. Pass through recently planted woodland, following a track climbing to the right to enter mature woodland through a gate.

6. On leaving the wood, cross a road and go through a gate. Cross a field (there may be a fence on the left) and continue to reach a track alongside a line of pines commanding the ridge.

7. Turn right and follow the track to reach a road. A commemorative stone to Maud Heath, with lines by the Rev. Bowles, stands here alongside a gate. To view Maud Heath's monument, cross straight over. More of Bowles' doggerel appears here. To find out more about this remarkable lady, we need to visit Kellaway's Bridge, where we learn from a commemorative pillar that Maud was a local widow

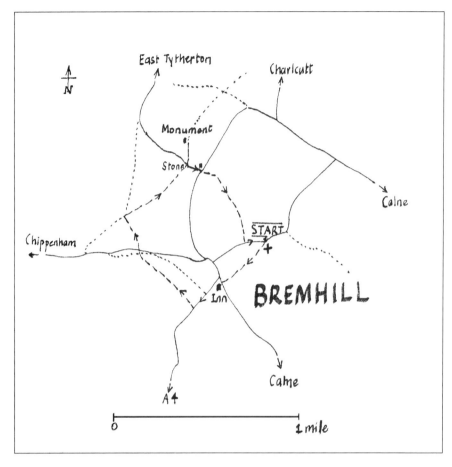

who in 1474 'did in Charity bestow in land and houses about Eight pounds a year forever to be laid out on the Highway and Causey leading from Wick Hill to Chippenham Clift'.

8. To resume the stroll, turn right, passing Monument Farm to reach a T-junction.

9. Cross the stile straight ahead (no waymark) and go over a field (Cherhill White Horse is visible on the horizon). Bremhill church soon comes into view. Keep to the right of a power pole to cross a stile in a hedge.

10. Cross a field, descending to a hedge gap on the right. From this point, a gate can be seen to the right of houses atop the slope ahead.

11. Descend on the line of the gate, cross a stream and climb to go through the gate.

12. Follow a drive to a road and turn left into Bremhill and back to the start.

Literary Connection

Reading the unremarkable verse of the inscription on Maud Heath's monument on Wick Hill or similar lines on the memorial to an old soldier on the outer wall of Bremhill church, it comes as something of a surprise to discover that their creator was once greatly admired by such eminent poets as Southey, Lamb, Wordsworth and Coleridge.

The name of William Lisle Bowles, vicar of Bremhill from 1804 until 1844, Prebendary and later Canon Residentiary of Salisbury, is virtually unheard of today. Yet the publication of his first slim volume of sonnets in 1789, inspired by a tour of northern England and Scotland, was greeted with national acclaim, the youthful Coleridge being so impressed that he wrote out forty copies as gifts for his friends. Later, Coleridge cited Bowles' influence as the factor that persuaded him to become a poet rather than follow his father into the church; Bowles was, he wrote 'a poet by whose works, year after year, I was so enthusiastically delighted and inspired'.

The Maud Heath monument, Bremhill

Once established at Bremhill vicarage, now Bremhill Court, Bowles set about giving the old building the Gothic treatment. He introduced a pierced parapet around the roof and added turrets and pinnacles to embellish the building. He then turned his attention to the grounds, installing any number of grottoes, hermitages, urns and miscellaneous fragments 'acquired' from the nearby ruins of Stanley Abbey, the resulting hotchpotch causing his friend Tom Moore to voice the opinion that Bowles had 'frittered away its beauty', adding that his sheep-bells were tuned in thirds and fifths. Despite his fussy innovations, his friend remained, Moore conceded, 'an excellent fellow notwithstanding'.

For many years, Bowles was a prominent figure in the literary-cum-social gatherings centred on Bowood, the home of the Marquess of Lansdowne. As well as Tom Moore and Coleridge, he knew Sheridan and Byron, with whom he eventually quarrelled over his life of Pope, and introduced the Suffolk poet George Crabbe, who had come to live in Wiltshire, into the Bowood circle. His prose works, meanwhile, and in particular his *Life of Bishop Ken* and *The Parochial History Of Bremhill*, were well received.

In later life, Bowles's nervous eccentricity, already apparent earlier, became more than ever a dominant feature of his character. Prior to his wife's death and his removal to Salisbury, he seems to have devoted much of his time and energy to writing doggerel verse and inscribing it on every tombstone, structure or monument he could lay his hands on. He is buried in Salisbury Cathedral and is commemorated by a memorial stone in the south choir.

Nearby Strolls

11. The Irish Poet's Last Home
Tom Moore at Bromham

Distance: 2 miles. A shorter option (1½ miles) involves retracing steps.

Location: Bromham. The village lies near the A432-A3102 junction, 3½ miles east of Melksham.

Park and Start: The village car park, along the main street

Maps: OS Landranger 173. OS Explorer 156. Grid ref. 964652

Terrain: Along pavements, surfaced and field paths, with one very short stretch of the A3102. The field paths can be very muddy after rain.

Refreshments: The Greyhound Inn

Route

1. Turn right along the street by the Greyhound Inn. At a right hand bend, turn left by railings down Stoney Lane (a surfaced bridleway). Cross a footbridge and climb along the woodland edge, ignoring stiles.

2. After passing beneath a bridge, notice a gazebo on the right, in the grounds of Nonsuch House. The bridleway continues as a drive. Follow it to reach a road (A3102).

3. For a view of Nonsuch House, walk along the path to the right. Nonsuch was the home of Ettie Meredith Brown (See Francis Kilvert at Kington Langley – page 37)

4. Back at the junction of Stoney Lane with the A3102, those wishing to avoid the main road stretch should retrace to the start. Otherwise, cross straight over and go through the 'squeezebelly' stile. Follow the grassy track to enter a field via a stile by a gate. Keep a fence on the right as far as a handgate.

5. Instead of passing through, turn sharp left across the field, aiming for a stile beneath a tree. Beyond, turn left along a grassy path to reach the A3102 once more.

6. Cross and turn right along the verge. Sloperton Cottage, former home of Tom Moore, can be seen on the right.

7. Turn left at a public footpath sign just beyond the cottage. Enter a

drive to reach a stone stile in a wall. Bromham church is now visible ahead. Cross a stile in a fence.

8. The footpath runs parallel to a drive on the right at first, eventually reaching a stile at the bottom right-hand corner of the field.

9. Follow the line indicated by the waymark to the left down the next field to cross a ditch and stile.

10. Climb to a marker post on the bank below gardens. Follow the line indicated up the bank to the right to reach a road leading to the main street.

11. Turn left back to the start.

No one should leave Bromham without visiting St Nicholas' church. The

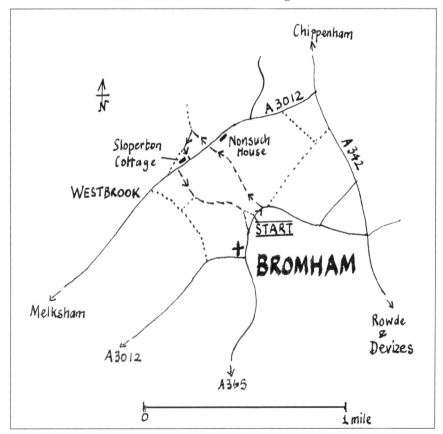

churchyard contains a memorial to Tom Moore alongside his grave and there is at timber lock-up by the churchyard wall. However, the most memorable feature is the Baynton Chapel, containing the tombs of the Tocates and Beauchamp families, richly decorated inside and out and dating from the late 15th century.

Literary Connection

It was in 1817 that the celebrated Irish poet Thomas Moore (1779-1852) was invited by Lord Lansdowne to take up residence near his country house, Bowood, at that time the greatest meeting place of writers, philosophers and scientists in Wiltshire. After having lived for short periods in London, Leicestershire and Derbyshire, and having lost two of their children in infancy, Moore and his wife Bessie settled for good at Sloperton Cottage, Westbrook, a hamlet of Bromham.

Bromham church

At that time, the cottage was smaller than it is today. It was roofed with thatch and was approached through pretty gardens along a gravelled walk. Its owner, and therefore Moore's landlord, was John Starkey, DD, who became a firm friend. From then on, Moore spent much time at Bowood, which was well within walking distance, and received a host of literary visitors, including William Bowles, Sydney Smith, Capt. Marryatt, Samuel

Rogers and Washington Irving. He was also on good terms with William Napier, who lived at Battle House in Bromham and who read chapters from his *History of the Peninsular War* to the Moores on his frequent visits.

Tom Moore's travels were, however, by no means over. In 1819, two years after moving to Sloperton Cottage, he spent some time in Paris and in the company of Lord John Russell, made his way to Italy where he visited Byron. Later, after Byron's death, he wrote a controversial life of his famous fellow poet and edited his works. Then, in fulfilment of a vow, he destroyed Byron's memoirs.

His native Ireland continued to lay claim to Moore's affection and seldom did a summer pass without him paying a visit. Following the publication of *The Epicurean* in 1827, he turned his attention to prose, including books on the lives of Sheridan and Lord Edward Fitgerald.

For all his literary success, tragedy continued to stalk Tom Moore throughout his life. In 1829, his sole surviving daughter, Anastasia Mary, known to the family as Stasia, died at Sloperton at the age of 15. Then in 1842, his younger son, John Russell ('Russy'), newly returned from army service in India, died of tuberculosis, aged 19. The Moores were now left with one son, Thomas, and he too, predeceased his father, dying in Algiers while serving in the French Foreign Legion in 1842, aged 28.

Tom Moore is remembered in Bromham churchyard by a giant Celtic cross erected in 1906, alongside his grave and that of his wife and two of their children. Inside the church, the west window commemorates Thomas, while the east window, by William Morris, with figures by Edward Burne-Jones, is in remembrance of Bessie Moore, and ranks among the finest examples of Victorian stained glass.

Nearby Strolls

The Parson Poet: William Bowles at Bremhill (page 41)

A Vicarage Childhood: Ida Gandy at Bishops Cannings (page 57)

The Dramatist at the Manor: Clifford Bax at Broughton Gifford (page 49)

12. The Dramatist at the Manor

Clifford Bax at Broughton Gifford

Distance: 2½ miles (short option: 1 mile)

Location: Broughton Gifford. The village lies off the B3107, 2 miles west of Melksham.

Park and Start: A small lay-by opposite the church, at the southern extremity of the village

Maps: OS Landranger 173. OS Explorer 156. Grid ref. 878631

Terrain: A mixture of pavements, surfaced lanes and field paths. Level throughout.

Refreshments: Fox and Hounds and Bell on the Common inns

Route

1. From the lay-by, walk into the village. On rounding a right-hand bend, the beautiful early 17th-century Manor House, once the home of the poet and dramatist Clifford Bax, comes into view.

2. On reaching the road junction at which the House stands, turn right along Mill Lane and follow it as far as Mill Farm, reached beyond a sharp right-hand bend.

3. Take the signposted footpath on the right, which passes between buildings to enter a field through a kissing gate. To complete the short stroll, cross the field, making for the church tower, clearly visible ahead. A kissing gate gives access to the road.

4. To continue the longer stroll, which necessitates retracing steps, leave the path approximately mid-way across the field to cross a stile and a footbridge on the left.

5. Cross another field, aiming to the left of a power pole, to reach the B3107 over a stile in the hedge. Cross with care to continue on the same line to reach a railway line.

6. The line is crossed over two stiles. Beyond, go over a narrow field to climb a stone stile in a wall. Continue over one last stile to the left, to reach the graceful little packhorse bridge spanning the River Avon.

7. Retrace steps as far as the footbridge crossed earlier. From this point, a footpath leads half-left back to the lay-by, reached through a kissing gate.

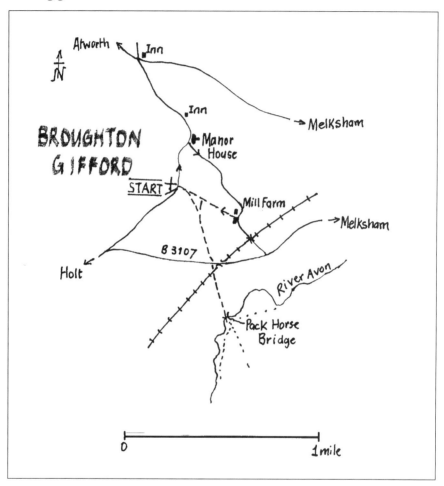

Literary Connections

Between 1911 and 1914, the beautiful gabled and mullioned Manor House at Broughton Gifford was the home of the author and playwright Clifford Bax (1886-1962). A younger brother of the composer Sir Arnold Bax, Clifford was trained as an artist but later turned to literature. His first play, *The Poetasters of Ispahan*, was produced during his time at

The Manor, Broughton Gifford

Broughton Gifford, and he went on to write many successful dramatic works as well as poetry, a novel, a monograph on Leonardo da Vinci and two volumes of memoirs.

One of Bax's passions was cricket and during August, his team of literary friends, the 'Old Broughtonians', took part in a cricket week, playing matches against local elevens. A somewhat reluctant member of this team was the writer and poet Edward Thomas (see 'A Soldier's Last Goodbye' page 74). Although his friend was only an indifferent cricketer, Bax held Thomas in high regard:

"As I learned to know him better I realised how raw was my literary sense by comparison with his."

Thomas often stayed at the Manor while engaged on his walking tours gathering material for his books and it was on one such visit that the two friends set off on a June evening for a stroll over the buttercup meadows and down to the picturesque old packhorse bridge spanning the River Avon. On that occasion, Bax recalled later, conversation centred on the poetry of Shelley, and in particular on his *Prometheus Unbound*. On a subsequent visit to this unfrequented stretch of the river, the friends were at the head of a picnic party and Bax recalled Thomas trying his hand at water-divining.

Other guests at the Manor during Bax's residence there included the author and poet Eleanor Farjeon and her brother Herbert ('Bertie'). Eleanor was to become a close friend of Edward Thomas and author of a moving record of his later life – *Edward Thomas. The Last Four Years.* Herbert Farjeon and Clifford Bax combined to compose a humorous poem about Thomas, aptly entitled *Walking Tom*, a gentle parody in the style of John Masefield, which caused much laughter among the circle of friends, not least to Edward Thomas himself.

Recommended Reading

Some I Knew Well, Clifford Bax, 1951.

Edward Thomas. The Last Four Years, Eleanor Farjeon, OUP, 1958. Republished Sutton 1997.

Nearby Strolls

The Irish Poet's Last Home: Tom Moore at Bromham (page 45)

The Botanist's Boyhood: William Keble Martin at Poulshot (page 53)

13. The Botanist's Boyhood
William Keble Martin at Poulshot

Distance: 2¾ miles (short option: 2 miles)

Location: Poulshot. The village lies between the A361 and the A360, 2½ miles SW of Devizes.

Park and Start: At the junction of Poulshot Road and the lane leading to the church at the south end of the village

Maps: OS Landranger 173, OS Explorer 156. Grid ref. 965589

Terrain: A mixture of lane, bridleway and footpath walking. The bridleway especially can be very muddy after rain. Level throughout.

Refreshments: The Raven Inn

Route

1. Facing the road, turn left and walk as far as a sharp left-hand bend. Turn right here along a bridleway (Broadway Lane).

2. Go straight ahead through two gates, following the byway sign. This is a section of the White Horse Trail.

3. As its name suggests, the track is wide at first, but narrows beyond the next gate. Eventually it joins another, wider track coming in from the left but continues its original course when this swings off to the right.

4. Keep straight on to reach a road. Turn right to meet the main street, with the Raven Inn on the left. Turn right.

5. To see the Old Rectory, where the celebrated botanist William Keble Martin spent much of his boyhood (1883-1891), walk along the left-hand green, passing the former school (now the village hall). The Old Rectory stands back from the road behind a picket fence, opposite the phone box.

6. To complete the short option, continue along the road back to the start.

7. To continue the longer stroll, retrace steps the short distance to reach a signposted footpath (now on the right) branching off from a drive to a house.

8. The footpath begins as a grassy track. It soon swings to the right to enter a field over a stile alongside a gate. Follow the line indicated by the waymark. Expansive views now open up away to the left and straight ahead.

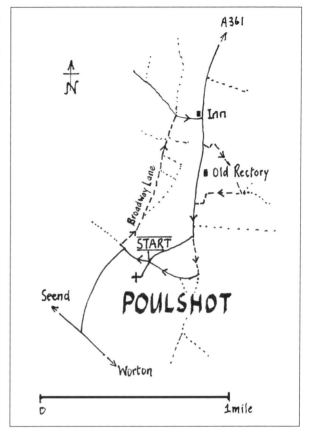

9. Go through a hedge gap and continue to cross a stile and plank bridge. 30 metres beyond the next stile turn right over a plank bridge and stile by a pond and keep to the right along the irregular field edge. Eventually, keep a fence on the right and cross the second of two stiles.

10. The footpath now crosses a field to reach the village street through a gate. Turn left.

11. A further alternative is possible on reaching a right-hand bend. Instead of continuing along the road, an option is to cross the stile on the left. Go over a field to a stiled footbridge and turn left along the farm track to reach Mill Lane. Turn right and follow the lane back to the start.

Literary connection

During the 1880s, a small boy could be seen searching the Rectory

The Old Rectory, Poulshot

grounds, greens and fields of Poulshot for the wild plants needed to feed the caterpillars he was rearing in cages supplied by a kindly uncle.

William Keble Martin was one of nine children of the rector. The family had moved to Poulshot in 1883 and was to remain there until 1891, when they left for Devon. During this time, William was sent away to school in Suffolk before entering Marlborough College, but he was able to indulge in his passion for butterflies and moths during the holidays and in time – 80 years in fact – this hobby was to lead to national fame through the publication of the most popular book on British wild flowers ever written.

But to return to Poulshot. In his autobiography, *Over the Hills...*, published shortly before his death, Keble Martin recalled with affection the boyhood delights experienced in this quiet Wiltshire village: watching the mowers, early on a midsummer morning at work beyond the rectory lawn – "Five scythes together in echelon across the big field and back again, sometimes deliberately missing nest of skylark or corncrake, with occasional stops for scythe whetting or for liquid refreshment."

Other early encounters with birds included searching for goldcrests' nests in the yew trees near the Rectory, witnessing a dispute between robins and redstarts for a nesting site in the wall of the nearby school, and discovering moorhens' nests on the numerous cattle-watering ponds in the corners of the fields.

But it was the fascination exerted by insects, and especially moths, that Keble Martin recalled most vividly from his distant boyhood. In particular, he mentioned the beautiful eyed-hawk moths that bred annually on the willows near the Rectory, the finely marked leopard moths, and the large red underwings that spread themselves in daylight on an old brick wall.

First at Marlborough, later at Oxford, William Keble Martin pursued his interest in natural history, eventually becoming a prominent amateur botanist. A career in the ministry confined his fieldwork to holidays and to snatched breaks away from his life's work. However, in 1965, his botanical skills were finally recognised by the publication of his *Concise British Flora in Colour*. This book, with a foreword by the Duke of Edinburgh, sold almost 50,000 copies immediately on publication and remains a firm favourite with many wild plant lovers.

Visitors to St Peter's church will be pleased to see that interest in the natural history of the village is still very much alive. A delightful *Wiltshire Country Diary*, written by Pam Langton and illustrated by Pam Mullings, is on sale in aid of an appeal fund to refurbish the church bells.

Recommended reading

Over the Hills ... W. Keble Martin, Michael Joseph, 1968.

The Concise Flora in Colour, W. Keble Martin, Ebury Press/Michael Joseph, 1965.

Nearby Strolls

The Dramatist at the Manor: Clifford Bax. Broughton Gifford (page 49)

A Vicarage Childhood: Ida Gandy at Bishops Cannings (page 57)

14. A Vicarage Childhood

Ida Gandy at Bishops Cannings

Distance: 3¾ miles

Location: Bishops Cannings. The village lies off the A361, 2½ miles NE of Devizes.

Park and Start: The north churchyard gate – limited parking

Maps: OS Landranger 173. OS Explorer 157. Grid ref. 036642

Terrain: A mixture of surfaced roads, tracks and field paths. Muddy stretches after rain. Gentle gradients only.

Refreshments: Crown Inn

Route

1. Walk through the churchyard and along Church walk. At its end, turn right (Horton sign).

2. On reaching a right-hand bend, go straight ahead along a concrete road to reach the Kennet and Avon Canal. Cross the bridge and turn left along the towpath.

3. Follow this for about a mile, to reach a bridge. Climb up to the road and turn left.

4. At the top of the slope, turn left by Harepath House along another concrete road.

5. Follow this road for half a mile. Horton strip lynchets (prehistoric cultivation terraces) can be seen ahead on the left. In spring, the calls of peewits and the song of skylarks relieve the monotony of the long straight road. Listen too, for the 'jingling keys' song of the corn bunting.

6. On reaching barns, turn left by the power pole along a rough track. Etchilhampton Hill rises impressively away to the left.

7. Go through a handgate and keep a fence on the left. Easton Hill, much loved by Ida Gandy, dominates the view to the right, while Bishop Cannings church comes into view on the left.

8. Go through a second handgate. The path now swings to the left by a

copse and becomes a good track down to farm buildings (Easton Farm) by a road.

9. Go over the stile straight ahead (signposted to Bishops Cannings 1 mile) to enter a field. The church spire makes a clear objective.

10. Cross a stile to the right of a gate and keep a hedge on the left to cross two footbridges.

11. From the clump of trees by a farm, the footpath heads across a field, in line with the church spire. Cross a footbridge and continue towards the church.

12. A stile gives access to a road. Cross this and retrace steps along Church Walk back to the start.

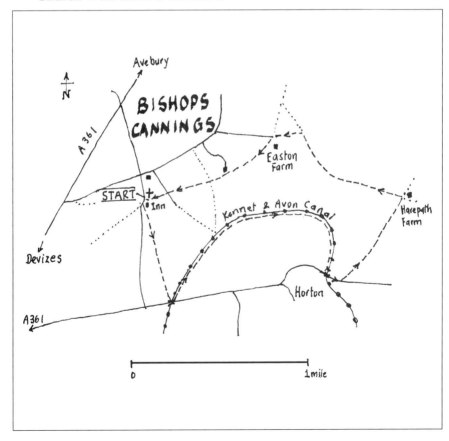

The Vicarage, Ida Gandy's childhood home, stands to the north of the church, overlooking the crossroads. Gabled, and built of red brick with a grey-tiled roof, it dates from 1863 and was the home of Archdeacon Macdonald, vicar for 47 years who, according to Ida Gandy, 'enriched Bishops Cannings with his scholarship and deep interest in its history and its people.'

Literary Connection

Though a comparatively small and scattered village, Bishops Cannings is notable for two reasons – its magnificent church and the writings of a daughter of its Victorian vicar.

Ida Gandy (1885-1977), daughter of the Rev Charles Hony, wrote *A Wiltshire Childhood* in 1929 and in so doing provided a valuable and delightful glimpse into a country way of life gone forever. Over thirty years later, and following the publication of two other books, *Staying with the Aunts* and *An Idler on the Shropshire Borders*, came *Round about the Little Steeple*, subtitled *The Story of a Downland Village and its Parson in the Seventeenth Century*, in which the author resumed her association with Bishops Cannings, this time presenting the reader with a well-researched yet highly readable account of the village's fortunes during a momentous period in our national history.

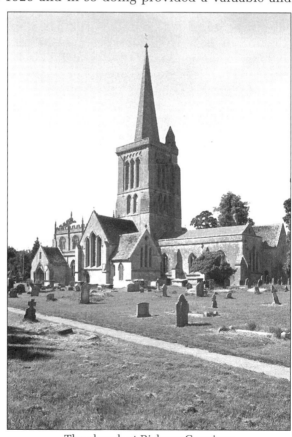

The church at Bishops Cannings

A Wiltshire Childhood, as befits its title, is a fond recollection of an expanding, exciting world, seen through he eyes of a young girl blessed with an amount of freedom enjoyed by very few children in late Victorian times. 'From very early years,' Ida Gandy wrote, 'we were encouraged to go unattended in the fields and over the downs.' Her mother, always unconventional, allowed her daughters to go barefoot through the greater part of the year: 'She urged us to be independent, and to take our own line through life, and if later on these lines did not always meet with her approval, she accepted them philosophically.'

Ida used her freedom well. Hers was an out-of-doors childhood, in which early explorations of the vicarage garden were soon extended to the neighbouring fields, and thence to the village itself, with its characters later lovingly recalled. In time, childhood expeditions saw Ida and her friends discovering the wonder of the downs, with which their village was surrounded on three sides: 'The downs were our own special kingdom and our passionate attachment never failed ... the little troubles and disappointments of childhood fell away from us when we had climbed out of the valley into that wide green country, and all that was adventurous and poetical in us swelled and grew.'

In addition to *Round about the Little Steeple*, Ida Gandy also wrote a history of another Wiltshire village in which she lived for many years. *The Heart of the Village*, subtitled *An Intimate History of Aldbourne*, provides an excellent introduction to this interesting north Wiltshire village.

Recommended Reading (All by Ida Gandy)

A Wiltshire Childhood, Allen and Unwin, 1929, Republished Sutton.

Round about the Little Steeple, Allen and Unwin, 1960. Republished Sutton.

The Heart of the Village, Moonraker, 1975. Republished Sutton.

Nearby Strolls

The Irish Poet's Last Home: Tom Moore at Bromham (page 45)

The Botanist's Boyhood: William Keble Martin at Poulshot (page 53)

Salisbury and Warminster Area

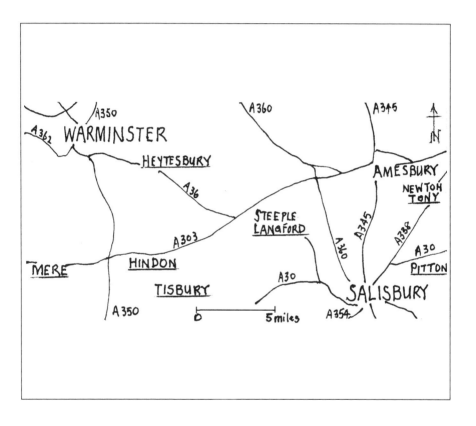

15. The War Poet Finds Peace
Siegfried Sassoon at Heytesbury

Distance: 2¼ miles (short option: 1 mile)

Location: Heytesbury. The village lies off the A36, 4 miles SE of Warminster.

Park and Start: Along the Tytherington road by the churchyard and opposite Mill Street, from which the stroll begins.

Maps: OS Landranger 184. OS Explorer 143. Grid ref. 925425

Terrain: Along minor roads and field paths, which may be muddy after rain. Level throughout.

Refreshments: Red Lion and Angel inns, Heytesbury

Route

1. Walk along Mill Street, opposite the churchyard gate. On reaching a left-hand bend, turn right to follow a public footpath sign alongside the River Wylye.

2. Cross a wooden bridge and in about 30 metres, swing to the left alongside a fence to pass through a kissing gate. Mill Farm, formerly a watermill, stands on the opposite bank of the river.

3. Continue along a gravel path and through another kissing gate to reach a road.

4. Turn right over a bridge and follow the road as it winds past Heytesbury Mill.

5. On reaching a right-hand bend, turn sharp left (Wessex Ridgeway sign) and follow the track as far as a gateway.

6. Swing sharply to the right here, as indicated by the waymark on a gatepost, and continue almost as far as a footbridge, which will be crossed on the return route.
   Note: To complete the short option, follow the last three route guides (11 to 13) below.

7. To continue the longer option, follow the waymark to the left between posts and keep to the right-hand field edge for about 300 metres, as far as a white marker indicating that the footpath crosses the field diagonally left towards the hamlet of Knook, visible ahead.

8. At the field end, keep to the right alongside the river to cross a stile and reach a bridge.

9. Cross the bridge and follow a drive, passing the Manor on the right, beyond which stands the church.

10. Retrace the outward route as far as the footbridge seen but not crossed earlier.

11. Cross this bridge and continue to reach a road. Turn right.

12. Keep to the left at a fork, following the winding road to a junction.

13. Turn right here back into Heytesbury. The church is on the left beyond the bridge spanning the Wylye.

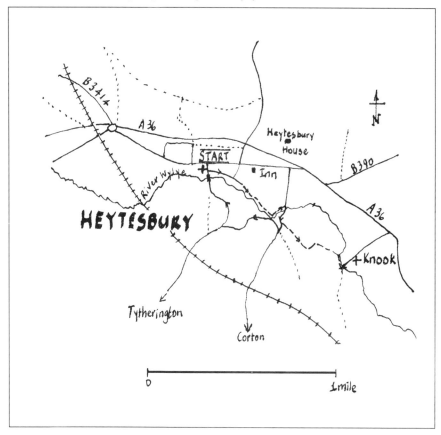

Former water mill, Heytesbury

Literary Connection

It seems strange that a wealthy poet, who risked his reputation – and indeed his life – in 1917 in protesting publicly against the continuation of a war in which he had served with distinction, chose to live within earshot of the military training ranges on Salisbury Plain.

Yet this is exactly what Siegfried Sassoon, then in his late forties, did in 1933, when he bought the spacious 18th-century Heytesbury House, which was to be his home until his death, aged 80, in 1967.

But contradictions abound in Sassoon's life, attributable to a considerable degree to the trauma of the war. Educated at Marlborough and Cambridge, he enlisted in what he then believed to be a noble cause, won the Military Cross for gallantry, and was wounded in action. Later, disillusioned by a conflict that he was convinced was being 'deliberately prolonged by those who have the power to end it', he embraced pacifism, and after the war became the literary editor of a newspaper. By now, his poetic gifts were fully recognised and in 1928, his largely autobiographical *Memoirs of a Fox-Hunting Man* established him as a prominent literary figure.

At Heytesbury, Sassoon's reputation, both as a poet and novelist, grew steadily. He had a wide circle of friends, including T.E. Lawrence, Stephen Tennant and Cecil Beaton, and was frequently a guest at the home of Edith Olivier at Wilton, where his hostess found him "by turns violently intolerant, sympathetically appreciative, and savagely satirical … He makes fun of himself as well as of other people and his descriptive powers are quite astonishing".

Riding, fishing and playing cricket occupied much of Sassoon's leisure time. His love of Wiltshire is revealed in much of his later verse, which includes poems inspired by such local features as Scratchbury Camp, Edington Hill, Heytesbury Wood and even the local railway station, a victim of the Beeching cuts. Sassoon was made a CBE in 1951 and awarded the Queen's Medal for Poetry in 1957.

Heytesbury House, to the north of the village, was converted into private apartments following Sassoon's death and is now virtually hidden from view from the A36 bypass.

Recommended Reading

Siegfried Sassoon, John Stuart Roberts, Richard Cohen, 1999.

Nearby Strolls

The Rural Rider's Return: William Cobbett at Steeple Langford (page 66)

A Wanderer in Wiltshire: W.H. Hudson at Hindon (page 70)

16. The Rural Rider's Return

William Cobbett at Steeple Langford

Distance: 1½ miles (flexible longer option possible)

Location: Hanging Langford. The village lies off the A36, 2 miles east of its intersection with the A303 at Wylye.

Park and Start: A lay-by on the Hanging Langford-Steeple Langford road, near the T-junction and Parish hall.

Maps: OS Landranger 184. OS Explorer 130. Grid ref. 037369

Terrain: Along minor roads, surfaced paths and tracks. The tracks may be muddy after rain. Steepish gradients.

Refreshments: The Rainbow's End, Steeple Langford

Route

1. Walk up to the T-junction and turn right by the Parish Hall.

2. Turn left almost immediately along a waymarked bridleway alongside Willow Cottage. The bridleway passes under a railway bridge, beyond which it climbs via a gate and is fringed by woodland.

3. Beyond the woodland, the bridleway joins another, climbing from the right.

4. The return to the Langfords is made along this second bridleway.

5. However, those wishing to extend the stroll, while at the same time enjoying sweeping views along the Wylye valley and beyond, will be richly rewarded by following the other bridleway as it climbs towards Grimm's Ditch and Langford Long Coppice. Although this involves retracing steps, the views, together with the rich flora alongside the track, amply repay the extra effort.

6. Back at the junction of bridleways, descend along the left-hand bridleway.

7. Cross a railway bridge and enter Hanging Langford. Cross the village street and continue along 'The Upper', passing a thatched cob wall.

8. The stroll continues along a surfaced path, with Woodland Trust woods on either side (open access).

8. Cross a bridge and continue beside the River Wylye to cross a second bridge, beyond which the path leads past the churchyard to reach Steeple Langford village street.

9. Turn right and soon right again along Duck Street. Two fine old houses, standing opposite one another a short way along the street, are worth noting.

10. Continue along Duck Street, passing lakes on the left, to cross the Wylye once more and reach the starting point at Hanging Langford.

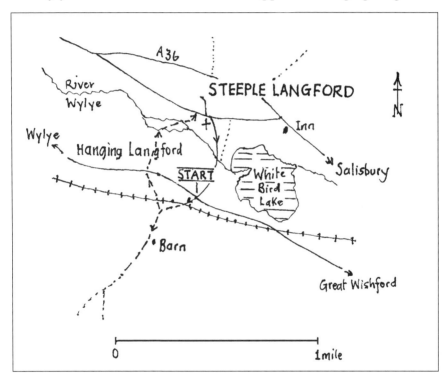

Literary Connection

It was the happy recollection of a childhood ride from his home at Farnham, in Surrey, to Steeple Langford, that prompted the journalist and politician William Cobbett to set out on one of his "Rural Rides" through Wiltshire in August 1826.

The 11-year-old Cobbett had reached the Wylye Valley after visiting Stonehenge and recalled: 'I went to the village of Steeple Langford,

Steeple Langford village

where I remained for the month of June till the fall of the year. I remembered the beautiful villages up and down this valley. I also remembered very well, that the women at Steeple Langford used to card and spin dyed wool. I was, therefore, somewhat filled with curiosity to see this Steeple Langford again.'

However, as Cobbett and countless others since lived to discover, a return visit to a place recalled with affection more often than not leads to disappointment. To begin with, the weather was exceedingly hot and as Cobbett's horse was being tormented by flies, he was impatient to find a public house with stabling. To his annoyance, Steeple Langford was without a single inn; not only that, but the church had lost its steeple – 'To which it owed its distinctive appellation' – and in short, Cobbett declared the village to be 'A much more miserable place than I had remembered it'.

Impatient to find stabling and refreshment, Cobbett continued his ride up the Wylye Valley. Incidentally, he failed to mention whether or not wool-carding or spinning were still being practised. And although, on reaching the next village, Wylye, he was relieved to find an inn, the beautiful garden he remembered seeing nearby 'seemed to be in a state of perfect carelessness and neglect.'

This is not to say that Cobbett found the whole of the Wylye valley displeasing. On the contrary, he wrote later that he considered the stretch to the north of Steeple Langford, and in particular the villages of North Bovant and Bishopstrow – 'sheltered in winter and shaded in summer by lofty and beautiful trees' – to contain everything he delighted in.

Recommended Reading

Rural Rides. Volume 2, William Cobbett, Several Editions.

Nearby Strolls

The War Poet finds Peace: Siegfried Sassoon at Heytesbury (page 62)

A Wanderer in Wiltshire: W.H. Hudson at Hindon (page 70)

17. A Wanderer in Wiltshire

W.H. Hudson at Hindon

Distance: 2¼ miles

Location: Hindon. The village stands on the B3089, 6 miles east of Mere and 2 miles SE of the A303/A350 intersection.

Park and Start: In the vicinity of the junction of the B3089 and the main street, from which the stroll begins.

Maps: OS Landranger 184. OS Explorer 143. Grid ref. 910329

Terrain: A mix of road, track and footpath walking. Tracks and paths may be muddy after rain. Gentle gradients.

Refreshments: Lamb and Grosvenor inns

Route

1. Walk up the no-through-road past the church. The road eventually becomes a narrow lane between high hedges.

2. At the top of the slope, turn right along a waymarked bridleway.

3. On reaching a cross track (drove road), turn right along it and follow it to cross a road. Good downland views now open up on the right.

4. In about three-quarters of a mile, leave the track, turning sharp right to follow another track, waymarked the Wessex Ridgeway. A steady ascent leads to a wooden gate.

5. The route continues between hedges (hard going through summer vegetation) to reach a road.

6. Keep left along this road back towards Hindon.

7. The Wessex Ridgeway branches off to the right through a gateway about 400 metres down the road on the right, to emerge on the outward route. However, this stretch can be virtually impassable after summer growth and walkers may prefer to continue to the junction at the foot of the hill and then turn right along the B3089 back to the village and the start.

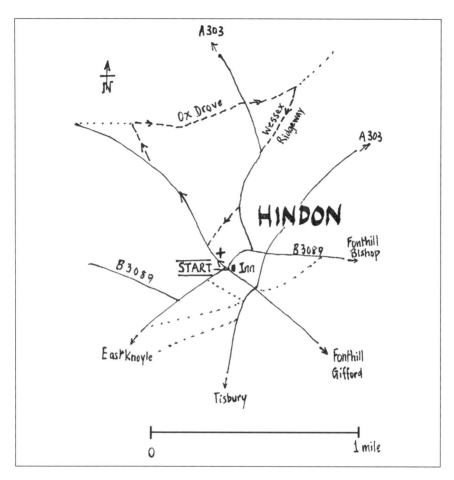

Literary Connection

During the spring and summer of 1909, a tall elderly man, the leanness of his face accentuated by a pointed beard, the severity of his expression softened by an alert and twinkling eye, was a familiar figure in and around the quiet south Wiltshire village of Hindon.

From his base at the ancient Lamb Inn, William Henry Hudson set off each day, in his cap and Norfolk jacket, sometimes on foot, more often on his bicycle, to gather material for his next book in the Wiltshire country-side he knew so well and loved so deeply.

Hudson had a number of books – on travel, birds and novels too – to his credit, including one on the neighbouring county of Hampshire.

The Lamb, Hindon

Indeed, the chalk downs and their associated river valleys held a special appeal for him and his descriptions of their wildlife, borne of hours of patient observation, had won him wide acclaim.

Hudson's new book, *A Shepherd's Life*, was to prove one of his finest. Its chief character, Caleb Bawcombe, was based on a real shepherd called James Lawes. It was set in an imaginary village called Winterbourne Bishop, which actually was Martin, over the Hampshire border. Hindon itself features prominently within its pages.

In the book, Hudson describes Hindon as "A delightful little village, so rustic and pretty amidst its green, swelling downs, with great woods crowning the heights beyond". He goes on to outline its colourful history, gleaned in part from conversations he had with an 89-year-old villager. This man could remember the years of agricultural depression following the Napoleonic War, when rioting labourers smashed the hated new-fangled machines. He had stories to tell too of the smuggling of wine and spirits, which flourished in and around Hindon during the early 19th century.

Inevitably, Hudson added to his store of encounters with birds during his stay at Hindon. Three different species – song thrush, pied wagtail and spotted flycatcher – were breeding in the ivy-covered wall of the

Lamb Inn and the elderly naturalist was joined by a number of the villagers as he watched the parent birds feeding their young.

Hindon's decline from town status, brought about largely by the arrival of the railway at nearby Tisbury, had taken place many years before Hudson's visit. Its public houses, formerly thirteen in number, had by then dwindled to the two still open today. To Hudson, however, this decline had brought with it distinct benefits:

"For although sober, it is contented and even merry, and exhibits such a sweet friendliness towards the stranger ... as to make him remember it with pleasure and gratitude."

Recommended Reading

The Shepherd's Life, W.H. Hudson, First published 1910. Many subsequent editions

Note: W.H. Hudson also features in a stroll in the Somerset section. See 'An Exmoor Explorer' (page 159)

Nearby Strolls

A Soldier's Last Goodbye: Edward Thomas at Tisbury (page 74)

The Schoolmaster Poet: William Barnes at Mere (page 78)

18. A Soldier's Last Goodbye
Edward Thomas at Tisbury

Distance: 3 miles

Location: Tisbury. The village lies on unclassified roads between the B3089 at Hindon and the A30 and is 10 miles west of Wilton.

Park and Start: Park near St John the Baptist church, from which the stroll begins

Maps: OS Landranger 184. OS Explorer 118. Grid ref. 944291

Terrain: Minor roads, tracks and field paths. Be prepared for mud after rain. Gentle gradients.

Refreshments: Choice of inns in Tisbury

Route

1. From the church, walk along the road towards the Crown Inn.

2. Continue past a roundabout and straight on up the minor road ahead.

3. Ignore a bridleway sign on the left at a right-hand bend. Instead, continue to pass a telephone box on a tiny green at a junction to reach another bridleway on the left.

4. Follow this past a house and through a gate. Good views now open up away to the left over the Nadder valley.

5. Pass through a handgate and descend a sloping field, keeping a fence on the left. Climb the opposite bank, keeping to the same line, to pass through a gate in a fence. Keep a hedge on the left at first.

6. Continue, skirting farm buildings, to reach a road fork at East Hatch.

7. Manor Farm, former home of Arthur Ransome, and visited by Edward Thomas when his daughter Myfanwy was staying here in 1917, stands opposite the road fork.

8. Take the left-hand fork and follow the lane, which descends between ancient hedges, towards houses.

9. Immediately before reaching the houses, turn left over a stile to enter a field.

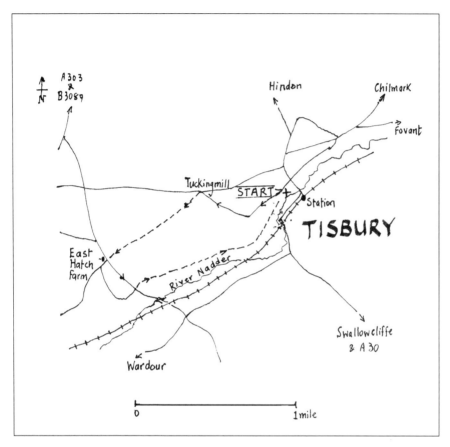

10. Keeping a hedge on the right, cross to pass through a gap in the far corner. Cross a fence on the right and go over a field, aiming for a power pole slightly to the right of a house.

11. Cross a stile between a house and a pond and follow a drive as far as a right-hand-bend.

12. At this point, keep straight on over a field to cross a stile in a fence.

13. Now follow the line indicated by a waymark over a field to a gap at the field end.

14. Beyond, climb a bank to a stile in a fence, then swing right along a hedge and cross a stile.

15. Continue to follow a track to the left of a house. Bypass a cattle grid, cross a surfaced road, and descend a field to a stile by a cottage.

16. Turn right now along another path, which soon follows a delightful stretch of the River Nadder.

16. On reaching a surfaced track, turn left along it and follow it back to the church and the start.

Literary Connections

Not even his idol, Richard Jefferies, or his friend and fellow country writer, W.H. Hudson, knew or loved Wiltshire better than Edward Thomas. Born and brought up in London, though with a Welsh father, Thomas married young and despite an Oxford education, found that the only way he could support a growing family was to undertake commissioned writing and reviewing – work which by its relentless demands confined his literary talents and undermined his health.

It was not until he enlisted in the army in 1915 that Thomas's true vocation – as a poet – finally emerged and it is for this remarkable late flowering that he is best remembered. However, one compensation that his earlier prose works had brought was the opportunity to travel widely in southern England collecting material and in this way he became familiar with Wiltshire.

One January morning in 1917 Thomas, now an officer stationed at Codford camp and awaiting embarkation to France, strode the ten miles over the downs to East Hatch Manor Farm, near Tisbury, where his six-year old daughter, Myfanwy, was staying with Ivy, wife of Thomas's friend, Arthur Ransome. (Ransome himself, later to achieve fame as a children's' author, was at that time serving as a newspaper correspondent in Russia.)

Seventy years later, in her book *Under Storm's Wing*, Myfanwy Thomas recalled that last evening spent with her father, "Safe and content in the crook of his arm." Father and daughter said goodbye the next morning and the little girl watched as Thomas set off back to his camp on a borrowed bicycle.

Later, in his diary, Edward Thomas described the return journey: "Such a beautiful ride after joining the Mere and Amesbury road at Fonthill Bishop – hedgeless roads over long sloping downs with woods and sprinkled thorns, carved with old tracks … a clear pale sky and but a faint sunset." Edward Thomas embarked for France the next day. He was

Street scene, Tisbury

killed by the blast from a shell at Arras on Easter Monday. He was thirty-nine.

Rudyard Kipling

The graves of John Lockwood and Alice Kipling, parents of the author and poet, can be seen by the south-east buttress of Tisbury church. Rudyard Kipling spent much time at his parents' home at Tisbury and is said to have written *The Jungle Book* while staying there.

Sir John Davies

The Elizabethan poet and politician was born at Chicksgrove Manor, east of Tisbury, in 1569.

Recommended Reading

Under Storm's Wing, Myfanwy Thomas, Carcanet, 1988.

Note: Edward Thomas features in a stroll in the Somerset section. See 'In Pursuit of Spring' (page 143)

Nearby Strolls

The Schoolmaster Poet: William Barnes at Mere (page 78)

A Wanderer in Wiltshire: W.H. Hudson at Hindon (page 70)

19. The Schoolmaster Poet
William Barnes at Mere

Distance: 1 mile

Location: Mere. The town lies off the A303, 6 miles west of its intersection with the A350.

Park and Start: Salisbury Street. Free car park at the eastern end of the town.

Maps: OS Landranger 183. OS Explorer 143. Grid ref. 814324

Terrain: Pavements and a variety of footpaths, which can be muddy after rain. Steep gradients to castle site.

Refreshments: Choice of inns and teashops

Route

1. On leaving the car park, turn left along the main street.
2. On reaching the Clock Tower, keep to the left and then turn left again along Angel Lane.
3. When buildings end on the right, opposite Fives Court, turn right along a narrow footpath, which winds round to enter the churchyard.
4. On the left is the Chantry House, where William Barnes lived and ran his school.
5. Leave the churchyard through the gate on the left of the tower and turn right along the narrow road. On reaching a corner, turn left along another path between St Anne's and The Close and follow it to reach a road.
6. Turn right, and in about 50 metres turn left through a barrier, cross a lane and immediately beyond a children's playground, turn left through a kissing gate and up a surfaced footpath.
7. When this path ends, climb two flights of steps on the left and continue along a grassy terrace, eventually climbing more steps to reach a kissing gate.
8. To visit the castle site, divert to the right. There are no visible remains of the castle, built by Richard, Earl of Cornwall, in 1253.
9. To continue the stroll, go through the kissing gate and follow the Long Hill ridge path – good views – which eventually descends to a stile, from which a path continues to a bridge crossing the A303.

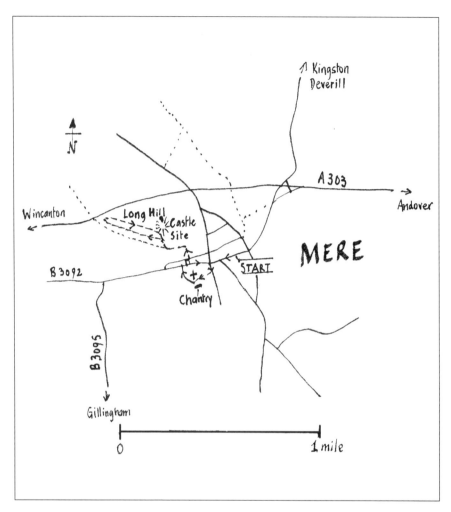

10. Instead of crossing the stile, take the path swinging away to the right. This skirts the northern flank of Long Hill.

12. About 100 metres beyond a gate, leave the path and climb steps on the right. This path leads back to the kissing gate passed through earlier.

13. Retrace steps down to the lane and cross straight over down a narrow path between walls to regain the main street.

14. Turn left along the raised pavement, passing the Clock Tower once more and continuing back to the start.

Mere from the castle site

Literary Connection

In 1823, a young Dorset man arrived at the little Wiltshire town of Mere, determined to better himself and thus be in a position to marry his sweetheart, Julia Miles, whom he had left behind at Dorchester.

William Barnes had raised enough money to open a little school in the loft of the Old Market House, which stood on the site now occupied by the Jubilee Clock Tower. He possessed an insatiable appetite for learning, especially languages, and was already an accomplished musician. He had studied geology and archaeology and had begun to write the dialect verse for which he was to become widely known.

The little school prospered and four years later, Barnes was able to marry Julia and move his establishment to the Old Chantry House to the south of the churchyard, which was to be their home until they removed to Dorchester in 1835.

Looking back on his life at Mere, Barnes described it as his happiest time. He wrote that he 'took boarders, gathering as best I could from book or man or any lore that was good for me as teacher or which I lived for its own sake.'

Later, Barnes entered St John's College, Cambridge, took holy orders and devoted the last twenty-four years of his life to the rectorship of

Winterbourne Came in Dorset. Here, in 1874, he was visited by the diarist Francis Kilvert, (see In the Diarist's Footsteps, page 37) who delighted in the old scholar's company, describing him as 'a very remarkable and remarkable-looking man, half hermit, half enchanter'.

However, it is to Barnes' daughter and biographer, Lucy Baxter, that we are indebted for a description of the Chantry House at Mere during her father's time. She wrote that it was ' a roomy old Tudor building, with large oak-wainscoted rooms, whose wide, stone-mullioned windows were entwined with greenery. It had a large garden and lawn, at the bottom of which ran a flowing stream, here widened into a pond over shadowed with trees … where William Barnes often came with his Patriarch in his pocket to pass a few happy leisure moments.'

Nearby Strolls

A Wanderer in Wiltshire: W.H. Hudson at Hindon (page 70)

A Soldier's Last Goodbye: Edward Thomas at Tisbury (page 74)

20. The Traveller at Home
Celia Fiennes at Newton Tony

Distance: 2¾ miles (short option: 1½ miles)

Location: Newton Tony (or Toney). The village lies off the A338, 5 miles east of Amesbury and 8 miles NE of Salisbury.

Park and Start: Near the church, from which the stroll begins

Maps: OS Landranger 184. OS Explorer 131. Grid ref. 218402

Terrain: A mix of quiet road, track and footpath walking. Gentle gradients only.

Refreshments: The Malet Arms

Route

1. From the church, follow the tree-lined lane out of the village, passing first a metal footbridge on the right, then Manor Farm.

2. A short distance beyond the last house, those taking the shorter route should go through a kissing gate on the left and follow the signposted footpath over fields to reach a woodland-fringe path. At this point, turn left to follow the longer route (5).

3. The longer route continues along the lane as far as a track (signposted 'road used as public path') on the left between barns and a former railway bridge. Follow this track, which eventually enters woodland.

4. On reaching a small clearing with another road-used-as-path sign, turn left (no waymark) to follow a clear path along the woodland fringe.

5. Approaching Newton Tony, the path dips to meet a drive. Turn left to reach a T-junction. The shorter route can be completed by turning left here back to the start.

6. To complete the longer route, turn right and follow the road for a short distance to reach a signposted footpath on the left, passing between houses.

7. Cross a stile into a field and climb with a fence on the left. When the

path levels out, aim for a stile in the trees ahead. Keep to the same line to cross another stile at the left-hand corner of the field.

8. Turn left along a tree-fringed path which eventually keeps a fence on the left to reach steps descending to a road.

9. Turn left down to the village. The church is on the right.

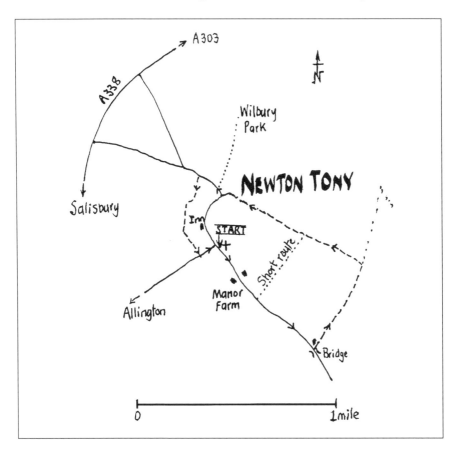

Literary Connection

It was not until 1888, two hundred or so years after they were made, that the journeys of Celia Fiennes first appeared in published form, imperfectly transcribed by one of her descendants under the title of *Through England on a side saddle in the time of William and Mary*.

A further sixty years were to pass before a carefully edited version of

Newton Tony

the journeys was published. Thanks to this edition, by Christopher Morris of King's College, Cambridge, we are able to follow the travels of a remarkable woman, whose achievements compare favourably with those of the celebrated Daniel Defoe.

Celia Fiennes was born at the long-destroyed manor house of Newton Tony, near Salisbury in 1662, into a family of staunch Parliamentarian sympathies. Her father, Colonel Fiennes, was the son of the first Viscount Saye and Sele and her mother was the daughter of another Roundhead colonel, Richard Whitehead. Little is known of Celia's earlier years but by 1685, when she set off on her first recorded journey, via Salisbury and Wilton, to the Isle of Purbeck, the 23-year-old was evidently a spirited and perceptive young woman with a lively interest in her surroundings, especially gardens, agriculture, buildings and manufacturing processes.

Until her mother's death in 1691, Celia seems to have commenced her journeys from the family home at Newton Tony. As well as the Isle of Purbeck, her rides took in Yeovil, Castle Cary, Bath, Faringdon, Banbury, Maidenhead, Windsor and London, reached via Hampshire and Surrey.

Following the death of her mother, Celia appears to have moved to London, eventually living in Hackney. It was from the capital that her later and more ambitious journeys took place and by the time she recorded the last of these, in 1703, she had not only visited every county in England but had also crossed into Wales and Scotland.

Considering the appalling state of the roads in the 17th century and the fact that the standard of food and accommodation offered by inns was often far below that to which she was accustomed, Celia Fiennes seems to have taken these privations in her stride. Fortunately for us, because of her determination to experience for herself and to record her impressions of the state of the country, we have an invaluable account of late 17th-century England as seen through the eyes of an exceptional Wiltshire lady.

Celia Fiennes died at Hackney in 1741, aged 79. However, her name appears on a memorial tablet on the north side of the nave near the chancel arch in Newton Tony church.

Recommended Reading

The Journeys of Celia Fiennes edited by Christopher Morris, Cresset Press, 1947.

Nearby Stroll

A Writer and his Roots: Ralph Whitlock at Pitton (page 86)

21. A Writer and his Roots
Ralph Whitlock at Pitton

Distance: 3 miles

Location: Pitton. The village lies off the A30, 6 miles east of Salisbury.

Park and Start: Near the church, at the northern end of the village, from which the walk begins.

Maps: OS Landranger 184. OS Explorer 131. Grid ref. 213316

Terrain: Chiefly along tracks and paths, with some minor road walking. Gentle gradients only.

Refreshments: Silver Plough Inn

Route

1. From the church, cross the road to take a surfaced path almost opposite, alongside a bus stop. Follow the path to reach a road.

2. Cross straight over to follow a signposted footpath, which climbs beneath trees and on to downland, which in spring and summer is rich in chalk-loving wild flowers.

3. At the top of the slope, cross a stile and go over a meadow to cross another stile. Now keep a fence on the right to cross a further stile.

4. Continue over a farm track and keep woodland on the left. Eventually the path enters the predominantly conifer Hound Wood over a stile.

5. Continue to join a wide track and follow it to the right as far as a signposted meeting of paths at the woodland edge. Here, cross a stile on the right.

6. However, instead of taking the direction indicated by the yellow waymark across a field, keep alongside the woodland edge to cross a stile at a corner.

7. Beyond a second stile, the path veers to the left and continues along the inner margin of the wood, leaving after climbing a bank to enter a field by a power pole.

8. Keep straight on, with a hedge on the left. Ignore a track, also on the

left, and continue, following the hedge as it swings first to the right then to the left, to enter a field via a metal gate.

9. In the field, keep a hedge on the left. The path becomes a track, which eventually swings to the left along a surfaced lane, passing White Hill Farm, where Ralph Whitlock spent his boyhood.

10. On reaching a road, turn right (beware – no verge) back into Pitton. The road descends through a steep chalk cutting before entering the village.

11. To return by the most interesting route to the church, continue past the Silver Plough Inn and the Methodist chapel, as far as High Street on the right, which leads back to the start.

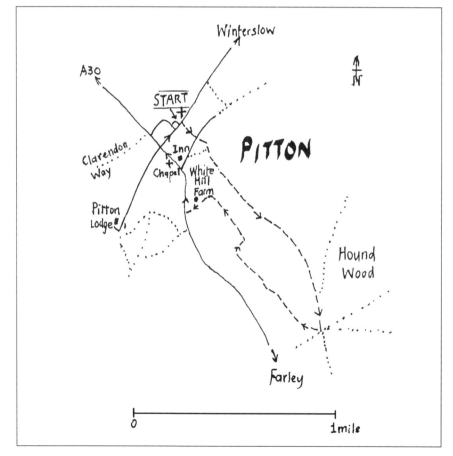

Pitton

Literary Connection

Ralph Whitlock was 18 when he persuaded the editor of a West Country weekly paper to publish a regular column of country notes. The year was 1932 and from these modest beginnings, Ralph, who had been forced to leave school two years earlier to help his father in his struggle to run the family farm during the years of agricultural depression, never looked back. In all, he wrote over a hundred books on farming, natural history and the topography of his native Wiltshire, as well as innumerable articles for a range of national newspapers and journals.

His versatility was remarkable. Following the second world war, he was commissioned by the BBC to write the radio series *Cowleaze Farm*, which proved so successful that it ran for seventeen years. He also appeared frequently on television.

A devout Methodist, Whitlock served for some time as agricultural consultant to the Methodist Missionary Society, travelling extensively on its behalf in Africa, India and the Caribbean.

Success in the wider world was never allowed to detract from Ralph Whitlock's devotion to Wiltshire, and in particular to that corner of the county around his birthplace village of Pitton. Always keenly interested in nature conservation, he instigated the formation of the Bentley Wood Trust to safeguard a tract of ancient woodland to the east of Pitton.

Needless to say, Pitton itself features prominently in Ralph Whitlock's writing. Two books in particular deal with the village in considerable detail. In *A Family and a Village,* he traces the varying fortunes of the Whitlocks of Pitton through the generations from their mention in the 17th-century parish register up until his own time. Later, in *The Lost Village*, he turns his attention to the village itself, which 'crouches in the last hollow of the chalk downs in the south-eastern corner of Salisbury Plain,' describing the changes which transformed Pitton in the years between the wars.

Although Ralph Whitlock spent the last years of his life at nearby Winterslow, it was in Pitton churchyard that he was laid to rest on his death in 1995, following a service in the Methodist Chapel.

Recommended Reading

A Family and a Village, Ralph Whitlock, John Baker, 1969.

The Lost Village, Ralph Whitlock, Hale, 1988.

Nearby Stroll

The Traveller at Home: Celia Fiennes at Newton Tony (page 82)

Somerset Strolls

Wells, Frome, Cheddar Area

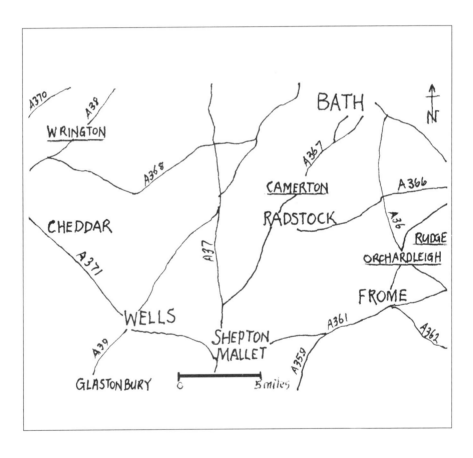

22. A Reformer Remembered
Hannah More at Wrington

Distance: 3 miles

Location: Wrington. The village lies midway between the A38 and the A370, 8 miles east of Weston-super-Mare.

Park and Start: Ample parking in the village, within easy reach of the church, from which the stroll begins.

Maps: OS Landranger 172. OS Explorer 154. Grid ref. 469628

Terrain: Along minor roads, tracks and fieldpaths that may be muddy after rain. A steady climb on the outward stretch.

Refreshments: Plough and Golden Lion inns

Route

1. From the churchyard lychgate, cross straight over the road to follow Church Walk into the village. Turn left (noticing the sign to Hannah More Close on the right) and beyond a garage, turn right along School Road.

2. On reaching a junction with a small triangular green, dominated by a lime tree, cross straight over to ascend Old Hill (no through road).

3. The surfaced road skirts Prestow Wood, climbing steadily, before becoming a woodland track, which eventually levels out, emerges from the wood, and swings to the right.

4. On reaching a waymarked fork, keep straight on, following the level track as far as a tree-fringed drive, swinging away to the right, opposite a large house on a slope away to the left. (Meeting House Farm).

5. Follow the drive as far as a gateway, beyond which the waymarked route passes to the right along a grassy path and follows the woodland edge.

6. On reaching a signpost, follow its direction pointer to the left into woodland. Leave through a kissing gate and keep a hedge on the right to reach a second kissing gate.

7. The footpath now turns to the left to follow a fence, then swings to

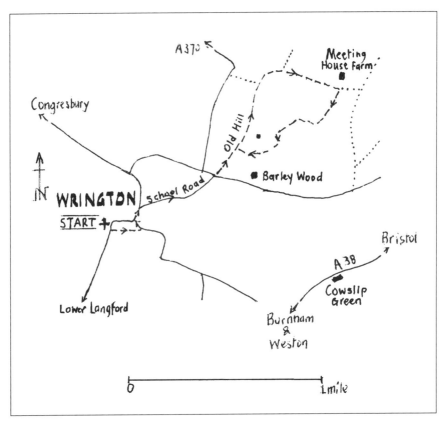

the right to reach and follow a drive to the left to regain Old Hill.
Turn left here and retrace the outward route back to the start.

Note: Hannah More's grave, shared with her sisters, can be seen to the
left of the church path.

Literary Connections

Few of the young Hannah More's intellectual and 'blue stocking' friends
in London in the 1770s – among them Joshua Reynolds, Doctor Johnson,
Horace Walpole and Elizabeth Montagu – could have predicted that
within a few years she would renounce the fashionable literary world to
devote her life to good works among the poor in rural Somerset.

Born near Bristol in 1745, the youngest of five sisters, Hannah was
educated in a boarding school run by two of her older sisters and learned
four languages. At 22, she was engaged to a wealthy gentleman, who

Wrington church

though breaking off the engagement, settled £200 a year on her. She determined to become a playwright and her first successful play, written in 1773, was *In Search of Happiness*, a pastoral drama.

Arriving in London, her literary gifts were soon recognised and two of her tragedies *Percy* and *The Fatal Secret*, were written for David Garrick. However, after Garrick's death, her enthusiasm for London life, and for the theatre in particular, waned, to be replaced by religious fervour. Encouraged by the anti-slavery reformer William Wilberforce, she retired to Cowslip Green, near Wrington, before later moving the short distance to Barley Wood, determined to establish schools in the mining and weaving villages, her aim being 'to form the lower classes to habits of industry and virtue'. Far from wishing to empower the poor, Hannah wanted to help prevent revolution, of the kind taking place in France, breaking out in England and to this end published a number of tracts designed to defuse revolutionary tendencies.

These pamphlets led to the formation in 1799 of the Religious Tracts Society, which undoubtedly helped to calm the situation, though leaving Hannah open to the accusation that she was feeding the poor on tracts instead of bread, and led William Cobbett, several years later, to brand her as 'That prim old prelate in petticoats.'

Her motives apart, Hannah More's zeal in establishing village schools in North Somerset ensured that the rudiments of education were offered to many children in 'a land of labour and vexation', long before the arrival of the National Schools.

On her death, aged 88, in 1833, Hannah More left £30,000, the greater part of which was bequeathed to various charities.

John Locke, the 17th-century philosopher, was born at Wrington in a cottage, now destroyed, which stood close by the church.

23. The Reluctant Rector

John Skinner at Camerton

Distance: 3 miles

Location: Camerton. The village lies off the A467, 2 miles north of Radstock.

Park and Start: Park in the church car park, signposted at the southern approach to the village. Note: The Old Rectory, former home of the Rev. John Skinner, is passed on the left of the drive leading to the church.

Maps: OS Landranger 172. OS Explorer 142. Grid ref. 686575

Terrain: Apart from a short stretch of pavement walking, the route is almost entirely along field paths, which may be muddy after rain. Moderate gradients with only one short steep climb.

Refreshments: No hostelries on route. Nearest inn (Camerton Inn) marked on sketch-map.

Route

1. From the church car park, walk along the path to the church. The grave of the Rev. John Skinner and his wife, marked by an urn on a rectangular base, stands opposite the porch.

2. Continue through the churchyard into a field and go through a kissing gate on the left. This gives access to a delightful walk through the grounds of Camerton Court. Pass beneath two bridges and leave through a gate.

3. Go half left across a field to reach a lane via a kissing gate and steps. Turn left to reach the summit of Camerton Hill alongside the school.

4. Turn right and walk along the pavement down into the village. Go over a crossroads (Carlingcott signpost on the right) and continue the short distance to reach a handgate, also on the right, leading to the Camerton Heritage Trail.

5. On the left, a statue of a miner stands on the capped shaft of one of the many collieries that worked in this locality until the 1950s. To the left of the statue is a display board and leaflet dispenser relating to the trail, which gives a valuable insight into the historical background of the area. **Note:** The trail is not included on the stroll.

6. To resume the stroll from the display board, cross a stile ahead to reach the road once more. In 20 metres, follow a public footpath sign on the right through iron gates and along a tarmac path between new houses to reach a crossways of paths.

7. The route now continues straight on through gates and to the right of a house to enter a field through a gate. Cross the field to a stile at the far left-hand corner.

8. Cross and keep a fence on the left to reach a stile near a house. Beyond,

Statue of miner, Camerton

keep a hedge on the right. At its end, descend the bank to join a track and follow it to the left.

9. The track swings to the right round a house and continues through a gateway. Immediately before reaching a bridge, cross a stile on the left to follow a section of the Limestone Link footpath.

10. On reaching a road, turn right and cross a bridge spanning the Cam Brook. Watch for a stile on the right alongside a surfaced road passing a conical-roofed pumping station.

11. The path climbs steeply to a kissing gate and up a field to Carlingcott, reached along a lane, which leads to a three-way junction.

12. Cross straight over, between the phone box and a letter box. At a

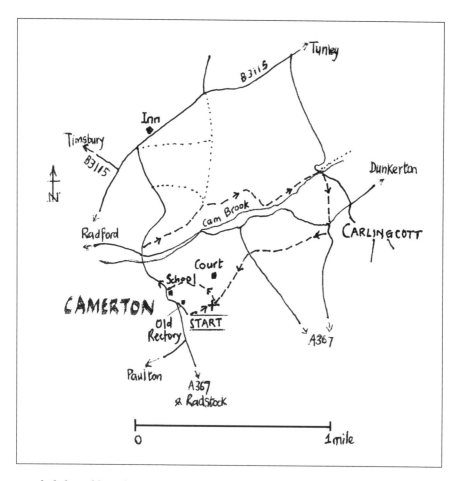

left-hand bend, turn right along a lane. At its end, continue along the right-hand edge of a field and follow the hedge round through a thicket to reach a stile in a corner with three gates.

13. Follow the line indicated by the waymark, keeping a hedge on the left. At its end, descend a steep field between two power poles, aiming for Camerton church tower. Cross a road (2 stiles) and follow the waymark line, with a ditch on the left, to a stile at the corner of the park boundary.

14. The gate into the churchyard, passed through previously, is straight ahead.

Literary Connection

If only John Skinner had pursued his originally intended career as a lawyer, instead of taking holy orders on leaving Oxford, the likelihood is that he would not have been driven to record anything resembling the sad and often harrowing events contained in the 146 volumes of journals which he left to the British Museum.

For Skinner (1772-1839), a sensitive, conscientious young man with an intense interest in archaeology and history, was totally unsuited and ill-prepared for the role of rector in a remote Somerset village, in which autocratic landowners, obstinate farmers and irreligious coal miners vied with one another to frustrate his every attempt at creating a united God-fearing community.

To make matters worse, personal tragedy struck hard and often. In 1812, following the death of his elder brother, his wife of seven years, Anna, also died, leaving Skinner with four small children. His one remaining consolation was his eldest child, Laura, and when, in 1820, she too died of consumption at the age of 14, the Rector's grief knew no bounds: 'How willingly would I have lived in poverty and parted with everything, could I but have retained this one treasure.'

John Skinner was to remain rector of Camerton for a further nineteen years, during which time his relationship with his parishioners, and eventually with his surviving children, became increasingly fraught. For a while, he sought relief from his woes in archaeology, carrying out numerous excavations in the surrounding area and in particular seeking to advance his long-held theory that Camerton, rather than Colchester, was in fact the site of Roman *Camulodunum*.

With the passing of the years, however, Skinner's journal became his sole confidante, until by 1834, his mental health had deteriorated to such an extent that he was reduced to penning a series of terse entries recording the unhappy ends of several of his chief adversaries. Finally, in October 1839, he shot himself in the woods behind his Rectory.

Recommended Reading

Journal of a Somerset Rector, John Skinner, OUP, 1984.

West Country Tour, John Skinner, Ex. Libris, 1985.

24. The Man behind the Masque

Samuel Daniel at Rudge and Beckington

Distance: 1¾ miles

Location: Rudge. The hamlet lies 2 miles east of the A36 at Beckington and 3 miles west of Westbury.

Park and Start: Near the Full Moon Inn, from which the stroll begins

Maps: OS Landranger 183. OS Explorer 143. Grid ref. 828518

Terrain: Lanes and field paths, which may be overgrown in places in summer. Gentle gradients only.

Refreshments: Full Moon Inn, Rudge

Route

1. From the road junction by the inn, follow the Berkley and Frome signpost. In 250 metres, just beyond a left-hand bend and opposite cottages, turn right through a gate to follow a signposted public footpath.

2. Keep a hedge on the left up a field, veering to the right eventually to cross a stile in a fence, followed almost immediately by another, this time of the stone-slab variety.

3. Cross a field, aiming for the middle of three trees, to pass through a gap in a hedge. In the next field, keep a hedge on the left and leave over a stile.

4. On entering the next field, aim for a cottage straight ahead. A gate gives access to Scotland Lane, the cottage being Scotland Cottage.

5. Turn right along the lane and follow it back to Rudge. Apart from farm vehicles, the lane is traffic-free and this allows a leisurely stroll, with time to notice the ancient species-rich hedges on either side, comprising hawthorn, blackthorn, elm, oak, holly, field maple, hazel and dogwood.

6. On reaching a T-junction, turn right. On the left is Rudge Manor, a handsome gabled house in a commanding position and believed to have been Samuel Daniel's last home after he retired from the court of James I.

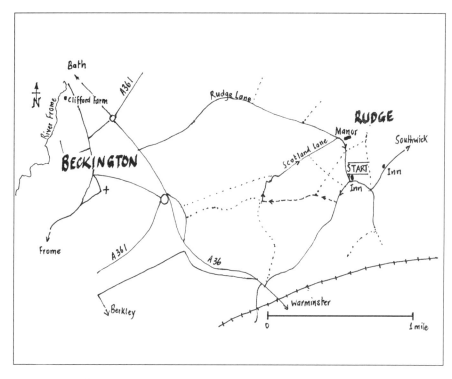

7.   The Full Moon Inn is at the foot of the hill.

Beckington: A short drive along Rudge Lane leads to the attractive village of Beckington, which is well worth a thorough exploration. Once famous for its woollen cloth, Beckington has a rich collection of gabled and mullioned houses and a fine church with a Norman tower. Within the church is the grave of the poet and dramatist, Samuel Daniel, together with a lavish monument on the wall of the north aisle.

Literary Connection

Born near Taunton, the son of a music master, in 1562, Samuel Daniel was educated at Oxford and after spending some time in Italy, was appointed tutor, first to William Herbert, Earl of Pembroke, and later to Lady Anne Clifford at Wilton. After the accession of James 1, he found favour in court circles, where in addition to composing songs and sonnets, he won acclaim as a writer of masques and pastorals for court functions, the most notable being *The Vision of the Twelve Goddesses, The Queen's Arcadia* and *Hymen's Triumph*.

Rudge Manor, near Beckington

Although his work is virtually unknown today, Daniel was held in high esteem not only by his contemporaries, including Spenser, Marlowe and Shakespeare, but also by later literary figures such as Hazlitt and Coleridge. He was a staunch advocate of the use of English speech and its natural modes and in his *Defence of Rhyme*, published in 1602, he openly challenged those poets favouring classical metres.

Towards the end of his life, Daniel retired from court to his native Somerset. He is reputed to have built a farm on the bank of the River Frome and named it Cliffords, after his former pupil, Lady Anne. A house of that name still stands north of Beckington today (see sketch-map). A few years before his death he is said to have moved the short distance to the hamlet of Rudge, where in all probability he built the handsome Jacobean Manor House featured on the stroll.

After Samuel Daniel's death in 1619, the monument we see today in Beckington church was set up by Lady Anne – by now Dowager Duchess of Pembroke – in memory of her former tutor and renovated by the poet William Mason in 1778.

As to his verse, the confidence he expressed in its survival has proved to be misplaced:

'I know I shall be read among the rest
So long as men speak Englishe and so long
As verse and virtue shall be in request
Or grace to honest industry belong.'

Elsewhere, however, he viewed his life – and his literary output – in a somewhat different light:

'....Yeeres have done this wrong,
To make me write too much and live too long.'

Nearby Stroll

A Patriot and a Park: Henry Newbolt at Orchardleigh (page 103)

25. A Patriot and a Park

Henry Newbolt at Orchardleigh

Distance: 3 miles

Location: Orchardleigh Park. The Park lies 2 miles north of Frome.

Park and Start: Lullington Lane, Oldford, on the B4090, 1½ miles north of Frome. From Oldford, follow the Lullington sign past a creamery. Park in a small lay-by on the left, a quarter of a mile beyond a narrow bridge.

Maps: OS Landranger 183. OS Explorer 142. Grid ref. 786510

Terrain: Along minor roads, tracks and footpaths that may be overgrown in places during the summer. Virtually level throughout.

Refreshments: The Ship Inn, Oldford

Route

1. From the lay-by, go through the kissing gate and turn right immediately, parallel to the road, as indicated by the waymark. Keep to the edge of golf greens for almost half a mile to reach a drive.

2. Turn left along the drive and in 100 metres, turn right at a marker post along a clear path. Pass through two gates to reach a road.

3. Turn left into Lullington. The church stands on a no-through-road on the right and is well worth the short detour to see. As well as a beautifully decorated Norman north door-

Norman doorway, Lullington church

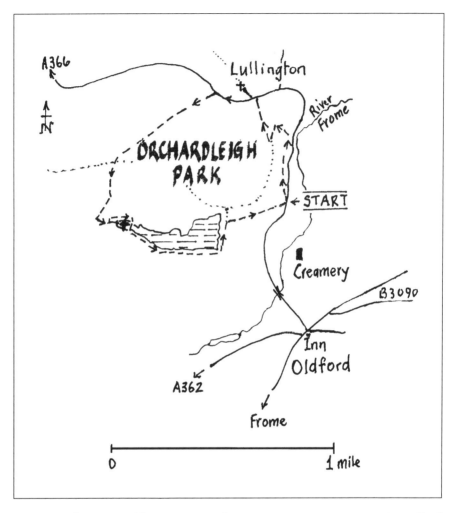

way depicting Christ in Benediction, it possesses a rare inscribed font dating from the same period.

4. To continue the stroll, walk through the village and on reaching a right-hand bend, carry straight on through a gateway (Macmillan Way marker).

5. Continue to pass through a gate and cross a field to a stile in a fence. Beyond this, follow the waymark half-right over golf greens to reach a drive.

6. At this point, follow the track opposite, signposted to the church. This is reached by a bridge over a moat.

7. In the churchyard, overlooking the lake, can be seen the simple little stones and crosses marking the graves of Sir Henry Newbolt and his wife. Notice too, the plaque on the church wall referring to the urn monument nearby to Azor, the much-loved dog of Sir Thomas Champneys, also commemorated in Sir Henry Newbolt's poem *Fidele's Grassy Tomb*.

8. To continue the stroll, retrace steps over the bridge and turn right through a kissing gate.

9. Keep to the right over a footbridge and go through a second kissing gate. The path veers away from the lakeside but eventually swings back to cross the dam.

10. In about 15 metres beyond the dam, follow the path on the left through bushes and continue round the eastern end of the lake as far as a waymark indicating right, immediately before a bridge.

11. This path keeps to the higher ground at first before descending to cross a footbridge. Beyond this, continue along the edge of golf greens back to the start.

Literary Connections

Although Netherhampton House, close by Salisbury in neighbouring Wiltshire, was where Sir Henry Newbolt spent the greater part of his life, it was at Orchardleigh Park in Somerset that he courted his future wife, Margaret Duckworth. The couple were married in the little church on the island in Orchardleigh Lake and it is here, in the churchyard overlooking the lake, that they lie buried.

Henry Newbolt, described by a fellow poet, Geoffrey Swain, as 'most English poet of our poet's Race', was born at Bilston, Staffordshire, in 1862, the son of the vicar. From grammar school, he gained a scholarship to Clifton College, from which he went on to Corpus Christi, Oxford, to study law. Called to the Bar at Lincoln's Inn in 1887, he practised law for twelve years. However, the publication of a patriotic novel, *Taken from the Enemy* in 1892, followed by a collection of poems entitled *Admirals All*, in 1897, convinced him that he was meant to devote his life to full-time writing and so in 1899 he embarked on what proved to be a long and successful literary career.

Memories of Orchardleigh, and especially of its 800-acre park, were to feature in Newbolt's novel *The Old Country*, published in 1906, thinly disguised as Gardenleigh. It is recalled with affection too, in his autobiographical writings: 'I bathed in the lake … it was like a bit of fairyland – glassy waters, kingfishers, silence everywhere – I was alone and felt like Adam in early days.'

As with the British Empire that inspired so much of his work, Newbolt's era has long since passed. There is no place in modern anthologies for the likes of *Drake's Drum, The Fighting Temeraire* or *The Old Superb*. And the poet who was knighted, made a Companion of Honour, and received honorary degrees from no less than six universities before his death, aged 75, in 1938, is recalled only among a dwindling band of poetry-lovers born before Hitler's war.

Nearby Stroll

The Man behind the Masque: Samuel Daniel at Rudge and Beckington (page 99)

Yeovil and Somerton Area

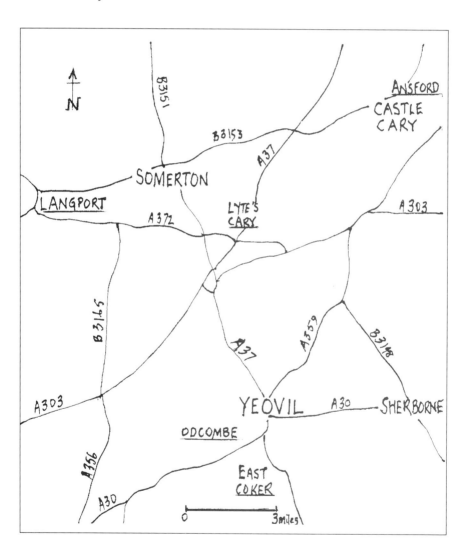

26. The Parson Diarist
James Woodforde at Ansford

Distance: 3½ miles

Location: Ansford. The village stands on the A371, adjoining the town of Castle Cary.

Park and Start: On Tuckers Lane, off the A371. Park by St Andrew's church, from which the stroll begins.

Maps: OS Landranger 183. OS Explorer 142. Grid ref. 638330

Terrain: A mixture of pavement, lane, track and field path walking, some of which can be very muddy after rain. A few steepish climbs and descents.

Refreshments: Choice of inns along the concluding mile of the route

---

Route

1. From St Andrew's church, climb Tuckers Lane to reach the A371. The large house on the right at the junction was the parsonage and former home of the Rev. James Woodforde.

2. Turn right, and in a short distance, cross the A371 to reach Maggs Lane (no through road). Pass a school on the left and continue as far as a sharp left-hand bend.

3. Turn right here, along a bridleway signposted to Solomon's Lane. On reaching this lane, turn left along it.

4. Follow this steeply banked shady lane to meet a road. Turn left, and in a short distance, turn right to follow a bridleway signposted to Ridge Lane and Hadspen.

5. The bridleway descends Knap Hollow, keeping a boundary on the left. At the foot of the slope, the path enters a small wood through a handgate.

6. The route now becomes a track (muddy after rain!) and continues as such out of the wood, swinging to the right to reach a road.

7. Turn right into the hamlet of Hadspen. Keep to the right at a fork and follow the winding, undulating road, passing a vineyard, to reach the A371 once more at a crossroads by the Waggon and Horses inn.

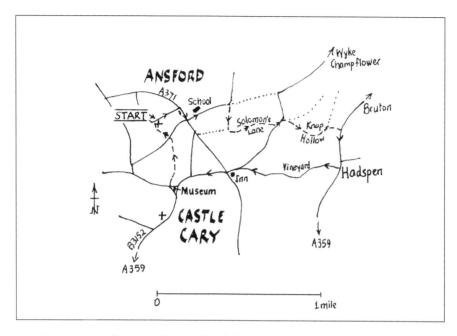

8. Cross straight over down the hill into Castle Cary. Ignore the first turn on the right and continue round a bend. Keep right at a fork to reach the Market House, which contains an excellent museum, with a room devoted to James Woodforde. Opposite stands the George Inn, mentioned in Woodforde's diaries.

9. To complete the stroll, turn right along Florida Street, opposite the remarkable Round House lock-up. When the street ends, continue along a path skirting a playing field.

10. This path eventually descends to a road. Cross straight over along Priory View, which extends as a footpath back to St Andrew's church and the start.

Literary Connection

Soon after the First World War, a collection of sixty-eight finely written notebooks came to light in a Hertfordshire village. On examination, it was found that they comprised a diary, kept by a Norfolk parson, James Woodforde, and covered no less that forty-one years, ending only with the diarist's impending death in 1802.

Selections from this remarkable diary were first published in 1924 and, since then, several other edited versions have appeared. As a result,

Round House lock-up, Castle Cary

the day-to-day doings of a comparatively unremarkable 18th-century clergyman have been brought to the attention of an ever-expanding modern readership, thus providing an invaluable insight into a way of life far removed from our own.

Until he took up the Norfolk living of Weston Longeville in 1776, James Woodforde lived for the most part in Somerset, the county of his birth. The second son of the vicar of Ansford, he was born in 1740 at the parsonage and eventually became curate of that village, and of neighbouring Castle Cary, after his father's death. A fellow and later Sub-Warden and Pro-Proctor of New College Oxford, he never married, having been jilted by the lady of his choice, and instead shared his home with Nancy, his niece, who remained with him until his death.

It is of course, the first section of the diary that covers Woodforde's life in Somerset, which in addition to his curacies of Ansford and Castle Cary, also included short spells in that capacity at Thurloxton and Babcary. Reading through these pages, we gain the impression of a man who, while dutifully devoting his energies to his calling, enjoyed his food and drink, details of the phenomenal consumption of which appear throughout. He delighted in winning a gamble, accounted for every penny of expenditure, lamented his aches and pains, yet freely acknowledged his failings. He gave regularly to beggars, and to all who were in need, and recorded with gratitude his safe arrival home after a journey.

All in all, the diaries offer a plain, unvarnished record of the day-to-day life of a rural parson – the finest of its kind to have survived the centuries.

Recommended Reading

A Country Parson. James Woodforde's diary. 1759-1802. Century Hutchinson. 1985.

27. The Herbalist at Home
Henry Lyte at Lytes Cary

Distance: 3¾ miles

Location: Lytes Cary (National Trust). The house lies one mile north of the A303-A37-A372 junction, 3 miles south-east of Somerton.

Park and Start: Charlton Mackrell church, 1 mile north of Lytes Cary

Maps: OS Landranger 183. OS Explorer 129. Grid ref. 528284

Terrain: Minor roads, bridleways and fieldpaths, which may be muddy after rain. Gentle gradients only.

Refreshments: Greyhound Inn, Charlton Mackrell

Route

1. Facing the church, turn left and walk down the hill. In a quarter of a mile, cross a stile on the left, to follow a surfaced track signposted to Kingsdon.

2. On reaching a bridge, follow the line indicated by the waymark over a gallop and across a large field.

3. At the field end, cross another gallop and go over a bridge spanning the little River Cary. Here, a waymark indicates right. Follow its line round the field edge for about 40 metres to go through a gate under a tree (no waymark at time of writing).

4. The route now crosses a field, aiming for a gap between woods. Go through a gate and follow the line of the waymark up to a gate by the edge of a wood. Go through the gate to follow a clear track as far as a crossways immediately beyond another gate.

5. Turn left by a barn down to a surfaced lane. At its end, turn left along a road and follow it to reach a T-junction. Again turn left. The entrance drive to Lytes Cary Manor is immediately on the right.

6. Beyond the drive, continue along the road for 120 metres (beware – no verge) to reach a bridleway on the right alongside the Lytes Cary sign (no waymark at time of writing).

7. Cross a field to a hedge gap and keep the same line over the next. In

the final field, keep a hedge on the right as far as a corner, then keep straight on to meet a wide track, Ridgeway Lane.

8. Turn left and follow this ancient way for about three-quarters of a mile to meet a road. Turn left. On reaching a three-way junction, follow the Charlton sign as far as a left turn, signposted to Somerton and West Charlton, just before a garage. The church is on the right, past the school.

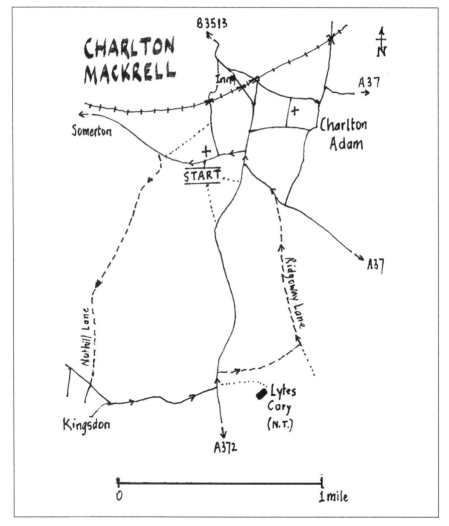

Lytes Cary Manor – Opening times

1st April – 31st October: Mon, Wed and Sat 2-6 p.m. or dusk if earlier. Also Fridays in June, July and Aug, 2-6 p.m.

Literary Connection

It was during his European travels in the 1570s that the Somerset gentleman Henry Lyte came across a copy of a herbal compiled by the Dutch botanist Rembert Dodoens. Greatly impressed, he managed to obtain a French translation of the work, which together with his own observations and ample references to the writings of English botanists, he fashioned into a book which he entitled *A niewe Herball or Historie of Plantes.*

On its publication in 1578, Lyte dedicated his offering to his 'most dread redoubted sovereign Queen Elizabeth', at the same time informing her that he was writing from 'my poor house at Lytescarie within Your Majesties Countie of Somerset'.

In fact, Lyte's 'poor house' was none other than the substantial manor house of Lytes Cary, established by his ancestors almost 300 years earlier and largely rebuilt by his own father. Wealthy and well educated, Henry Lyte was able to devote his time and energy to the botanical and horticultural activities close to his heart and his observations on the flora of his locality, though fairly sparse, nonethe-

The church at Charlton Mackrell

less reveal him to have been a capable botanist, while his lists of local names for both wild and garden flowers make delightful reading.

In 1588, ten years after the publication of his herbal, Henry Lyte brought out another book, *The Light of Britayne: A Recorde of the honourable originall and Antiquitie of Britaine*. Unlike the herbal, which had been eagerly received, Lyte's attempt at a national history failed to capture the public interest and was soon forgotten.

A similar fate was to befall Henry Lyte himself. Together with his wives and children, he was buried in the north transept of Charlton Mackrell church but following a drastic 19th-century restoration, the Lyte monuments seem to have disappeared and his herbal serves as the sole reminder of his life.

Lytes Cary Manor was itself under threat during the early years of the 20th century. Dilapidated and serving in part as a farm, it was bought by Sir Walter Jenner, grandson of the famous physician, and sensitively restored. Now the property of the National Trust, it is visited and admired by thousands each year and its delightful gardens, with their Elizabethan hedges, plants and trees, would surely have pleased Henry Lyte too.

Nearby Stroll

The Versatile Victorian: Walter Bagehot at Langport (page 116)

28. The Versatile Victorian
Walter Bagehot at Langport

Distance: 1¼ miles

Location: Langport. The town stands at the junction of the A372 and A378, 10 miles NW of Yeovil.

Park and Start: Cocklemoor free car park near library and TIC

Maps: OS Landranger 193. OS Explorer 129. Grid ref. 420268

Terrain: A mixture of pavements and footpaths. One steepish climb at the beginning of the stroll.

Refreshments: Choice of inns at Langport

Route

1. From the library entrance, climb the steep hill, Whatley Lane, on the left. The testing gradient rewards with views of the town.

2. Pass through a barrier and bear right at the top of the slope. Some of the town's most distinctive houses, mainly 18th century, now come into view.

3. Dominating the scene is the elegant embattled and pinnacled tower of All Saints' Church. The Bagehot graves, including that of the celebrated Walter – economist, critic and authority on the Constitution – are in the far left-hand corner of the graveyard, behind the church.

4. Continue past the church to reach the so-called Hanging Chapel, standing above an archway spanning the road. This is reputed to date from the early 14th century and has served as town hall, school, museum and Masonic lodge.

5. Below the Hanging Chapel and opposite a new development, Orchard Vale, turn down a public footpath and go through a kissing gate at the foot of the slope.

6. Now turn left to cross a stile and follow a stream. Go through a gate and turn right along a lane signposted to Hurd's Hill.

7. Immediately before reaching Huish Bridge over the River Parrett (from which a view can be had of the town) a footpath on the right leads back into Langford, alongside a catchwater at first, known as Back River, and then over a bridge and along a surfaced path back to the car park and the start.

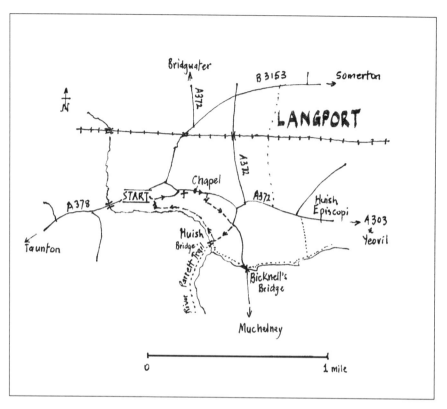

Literary Connection

When an eminent biographer describes his subject as 'Victorian England's most versatile genius', there can be little doubt that an exceptional person is under discussion. And when we discover that this man, born, bred and buried in a little Somerset town, achieved in his short life – he died at fifty-one – distinction as a political economist, historian and literary critic, we begin to appreciate why the people of Langport are proud of their town's most famous son, Walter Bagehot.

Born in 1826, the son of a Langport banker, Bagehot was educated at University College, London and called to the Bar. He soon realised that a career in law was not for him, however, and he joined Stuckey's, his father's bank. His grasp of banking and of economics generally, was quickly attained and soon he was writing articles on a range of subjects and by 1860 was editing *The Economist*. His career now took him to London but he never lost touch with his Langport roots, returning often

Walter Bagehot's grave

to the town. In 1867 he published what to many was his greatest work, *The English Constitution,* which was translated into several languages. This was followed by another much-praised work, *Physics and Politics.* His book, *Literary Studies,* was published posthumously.

As well as his grave in All Saints' churchyard, featured on the stroll, Bagehot's birthplace, Bank House, next to the Langport Arms, bears a commemorative stone, while on rising ground to the west of the town stands Herd's Hill, the great man's former home, where he died in 1877.

Nearby Stroll

The Herbalist at Home: Henry Lyte at Lytes Cary (page 112)

29. The Walking Wonder

Thomas Coryate at Odcombe

Distance: 3¾ miles

Location: Odcombe. The village lies between the A3088 and the A30, 3 miles west of Yeovil.

Park and Start: Near the church, from where the stroll begins

Maps: OS Landranger 194. OS Explorer 129. Grid ref. 507154

Terrain: Along minor roads, tracks and field paths, some of which may be muddy after rain. One steepish climb, otherwise fairly level.

Refreshments: Mason's Arms

Route

1. Facing the church, turn right and walk to the crossroads. Turn right. In 100 metres, turn left along a lane.

2. Pass to the right of farm buildings to follow a track. On reaching another, wider track, turn left along it.

3. When this track divides, take the right-hand fork along Hockers Hill. This ancient way burrows between hedges, with glimpses away to the right of distant wooded slopes.

4. The route passes an old boundary stone on the left of the track. Beyond a gateway on the right, the track widens. In 100 metres after the gateway, watch for a marker post on the bank on the left, indicating a public footpath swinging sharply to the left.

5. Take this path and in 20 metres, climb a bank to pass through a kissing gate and follow the line indicated by the waymark along the hedge side to the left.

6. The path eventually descends to Bagnell Farm. Go through the gate to the right of the house on the left and on to pass through another.

7. Now follow the line indicated by the waymark up a steep field. At the top, pass through a gateway and follow a grassy track through a gate and on to reach a lane.

8. Turn left and follow the lane to a shady T-junction. (Stump Stone on sketch-map.) Turn left and right at the next junction.

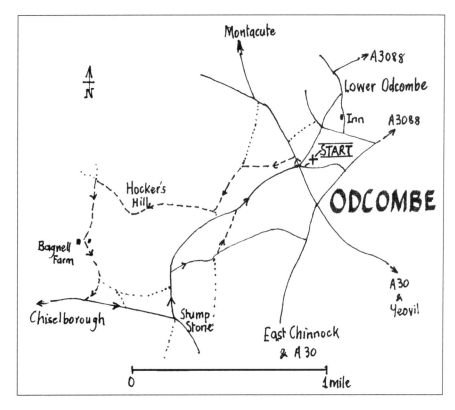

9. In ¼ mile, leave the lane at a lay-by on the left to follow a waymarked footpath across two fields to reach Street lane.

10. Turn right into Odcombe. The church can be seen ahead.

Literary Connection

The representation of a pair of shoes and other exhibits on display in the church of St Peter and St Paul in Odcombe are reminders that the village was the birthplace of Thomas Coryate, pioneer tourist and author of *Coryate's Crudities*, published in 1611 and the first guide book to foreign parts written in English.

The son of the village rector, Coryate was born about 1577 and despite receiving an Oxford education, seems to have made his name originally as a kind of court jester to Henry, Prince of Wales. However, contemporaries such as Ben Jonson were quick to recognise his ready wit and skill with words and cannot have been surprised when Coryate tired of clowning and sought other means to channel his restless energy.

Tom Coryate's shoes

And so, in 1608, Tom Coryate set out from Dover for Calais on what proved to be a remarkable tour, much of it on foot. In five months he is said to have covered almost 2,000 miles, passing through France, Italy, Switzerland, Germany and the Netherlands, noting as he went 'Beautifull Cities, gorgeous Palaces, impregnable Castles and Fortresses, Towers piercing in a manner up to the Cloudes, fertile territories replenished with a very Cornucopia of all manner of commodities...'

Of all the sights that delighted his keenly observant eye, Venice claimed the crown. He calculated the distance from there to Odcombe ('my sweet native soil') as 952 miles and on his return hung his shoes in the nave of the church, where they remained for almost a hundred years.

Coryate spent the next three years writing his book, which he promoted under his self-mocking nickname of 'The Odcombian Legge-Stretcher'. It was well received and its author amassed an impressive collection of testimonials, many by celebrated literary figures, including Ben Jonson, Michael Drayton, Thomas Campion and John Donne.

Meanwhile, two hitherto unknown artefacts Coryate brought back from his travels – the table fork and the parasol – soon became widely used in English society.

In 1612, Tom Coryate set off once more for foreign parts, this time intent on an even more ambitious and lengthy tour to include Greece, Palestine, Persia and India. Again travelling mainly on foot, he studied the languages of the lands through which he passed, sent letters home, and kept a journal of his travels. In 1617, however, he caught dysentery at Surat in India and died there, aged forty.

Recommended Reading
Shanks' Pony, Morris Marples, 1960.

Nearby Stroll
A Pirate, a Poet and a Poem: T.S. Eliot at East Coker (page 122)

30. A Pirate, a Poet and a Poem

T.S. Eliot at East Coker

Distance: 2¾ miles (short option: 2 miles)

Location: East Coker. The village lies midway between the A30 and the A37, 2 miles SW of Yeovil.

Park and Start: By the almshouses on the road leading to the church and Court

Maps: OS Landranger 194. OS Explorer 129. Grid ref. 539123

Terrain: Chiefly along tracks and field paths. Gentle gradients only.

Refreshments: Helyar Arms

Route

1. From the almshouses, walk up towards the church and on reaching the gates, turn right along the lane.

2. At its end, where a drive swings sharply to the left opposite cottages, continue straight on through a kissing gate and along the tree-lined path, signposted to Primrose Hill.

3. Follow this path to reach a road and cross straight over along a no-through-road.

4. The road continues as a surfaced track beyond Westfield Farm. When it swings sharply to the right, go straight on, soon turning left by woodland to reach a T-junction of paths by a house.

5. Follow the Upper Sleights sign to the left. Cross a stile into a field and keep a hedge on the left. Good views now open up away to the right.

6. Leave the field through a handgate and follow the line indicated by the waymark over the next field to reach a road via a stile, about 30 metres to the right of a house.

7. Turn right downhill. On reaching a junction, turn first left, along Isles Lane.

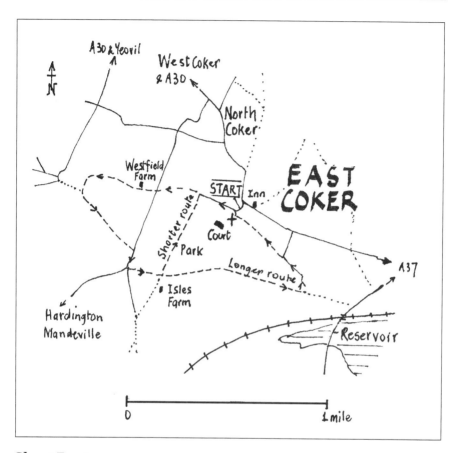

Short Route

8a. Opposite the turning to Isles Farm on the right, climb steps into Sleights plantation (Coker Court Park signpost).

9a. Leave the wood over a stile and follow the line indicated by the waymark over the park to cross a stile by a gate.

10a. Keep a fence on the right down the field to rejoin the outward route at the cottages passed earlier. Turn right back to the start.

Longer Route

8. Follow Isles Lane for about three-quarters of a mile past the farm to reach a lane on the left with houses visible beyond.

9. Turn left at the foot of the lane and go straight on at a right-hand bend, passing between gate pillars and through a kissing gate.

10. The path passes farm buildings on the right and eventually keeps a wall on the right to reach the church path through a kissing gate.

11. Turn right back to the start.

Literary Connection

Until the 1930s, the only claim to fame of which the villagers of East Coker could boast was that the navigator, geographer – and later, buccaneer – William Dampier, had been born there in 1652.

However, in 1936, the American-born poet Thomas Stearns Eliot, having established that his ancestor, Andrew Eliot, had emigrated from

the village in the 17th century, visited East Coker and subsequently gave its name to the second section of his celebrated *Four Quartets*, which was published in 1944.

T.S. Eliot was not the first descendant of Andrew Eliot to make his mark in America. The Eliots had long been a distinguished Boston family, one of whom had been the founder of Washington University. However, T.S. Eliot's future was destined to lie in England; he entered Oxford in 1914, served for a time as a teacher, then entered banking, a career which he was to follow for many years until he was able to devote his life to literature.

East Coker church

We have no means of knowing the exact impression East Coker made on the middle-aged poet on his first visit in 1936. One eminent writer, visiting some twenty-odd years earlier, had described it as 'as pretty a place as there is', and today, wandering along its street of Ham Hill stone houses, it would be hard to disagree with that verdict.

That the village's associations meant much to the poet, however, there can be no doubt. In accordance with his wishes, on his death, aged 76, in 1965, his ashes were interred in St Michael's churchyard and a memorial tablet was erected within the church in his honour.

And so, this Somerset village lays claim to arguably the 20th century's greatest poet, winner of the Nobel Prize for Literature, who became a naturalised British subject and who ensured a place for the village of his ancestors in the annals of literature.

The Quantocks Area

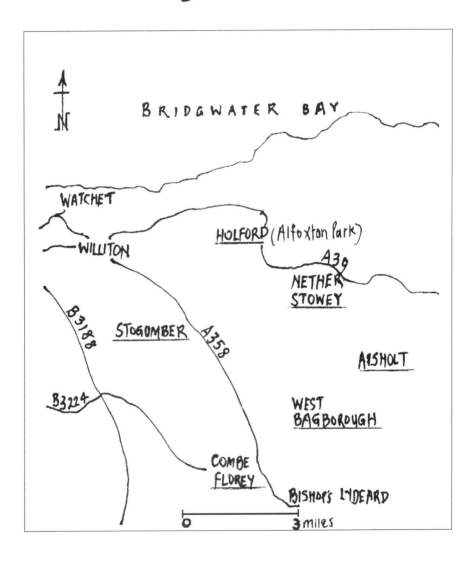

31. A Quantock Year
The Wordsworths at Alfoxton Park

Distance: 2½ miles

Location: Holford. The village lies off the A39 between Williton and Nether Stowey.

Park and Start: In the official car park

Directions: Approaching from Bridgwater, leave the A39 along the first of two lanes on the left, almost opposite a bus shelter. Pass the church on the left and follow the winding lane. The tree-shaded Bowling Green car park is on the left.

Maps: OS Landranger 181. OS Explorer 140. Grid ref. 155411

Terrain: Along surfaced minor roads and stony tracks. Some mud after rain. Some steepish gradients.

Refreshments: Nearest inns at Kilve and Nether Stowey

Route

1. On leaving the car park, turn left along the surfaced road and follow it round a sharp right-hand bend, at which stands an ancient dog pound bearing the crest of the St Albyns, former owners of Alfoxton Park.

2. Continue along the road, which eventually swings to the left, offering extensive sea views.

3. Keep on beyond a cattle grid, passing the entrance to the House (now a hotel) on the left.

4. Pass another cattle grid and keep on round a right-hand bend, passing a youth hostel sign on the right.

5. The road now swings to the left to pass Alfoxton Cottage and reach a meeting of routes.

6. Take the rough track ahead, passing a 'no vehicles' sign. Follow this climbing track for about a quarter of a mile, as far as another track dipping away to the left.

7. Take this track down to a meeting of tracks by fire beaters.

8. At this point, take the wide track, formerly known as the Great Road,

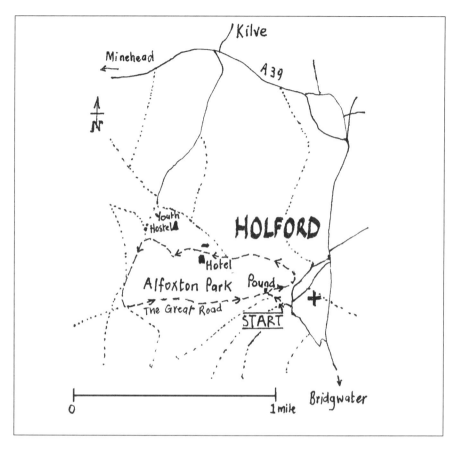

which linked Bridgwater and Minehead. This leads into woodland.
Follow it for about three quarters of a mile past giant veteran beeches
down to join the modern road by the dog pound passed on the outward route.

9. Retrace steps to the start.

Literary Connections

It was through their friendship with Samuel Taylor Coleridge that William Wordsworth and his sister Dorothy moved from Dorset to live in the
Quantocks in July 1797. Coleridge's friend, Tom Poole of Nether Stowey,
persuaded Mrs St Albyn, owner of the nearby Georgian house, Alfoxden
Park (now spelt Alfoxton) to lease it to the Wordsworths for an annual
rent of £23 and for almost a year the Wordsworths and Coleridge met on

Veteran beech, Holford

most days, walked and talked together, and established an affinity that yielded fine poetry and a remarkable journal – the fruits of 'Three persons and one soul'.

And although his Quantock period was one of Wordsworth's most productive – he wrote no less than nineteen poems for inclusion in *Lyrical Ballads*, his joint venture with Coleridge – it is to his sister Dorothy that we are most indebted for her impressions of that time, recorded in her Alfoxden Journal. Begun at the instigation of her brother, who copied the first entry into his own notebook and may

well have made use of its contents when composing his verses, Dorothy's surviving journal is a tantalising fragment of the original, which disappeared some time after parts of it were transcribed and published by William Knight in 1897.

What remains are a mere fourteen pages of the journal, covering the four months January to May 1798, written when Dorothy was twenty-six. For all their brevity, the entries reveal a woman of deep sensitivity and literary skill, whose love of nature and outdoor life was exceeded only by her utter devotion to her brother. Coleridge was quick to recognise these qualities in his friend's 'exquisite sister', remarking on 'her eye watchful in minutest observation of nature'.

It makes an absorbing, if somewhat frustrating exercise attempting to trace the walks undertaken by the Wordsworths and Coleridge from the Journal, using an Ordnance Survey map. For apart from the well-worn route between Alfoxden and Nether Stowey, Dorothy seldom gives precise locations, contenting herself merely to leave the hills, woods, and coombes unnamed, instead concentrating on her impressions of views, wild life and weather conditions.

Unfortunately, the trio's wanderings, often after nightfall, aroused the suspicions of the local people, who alerted government agents in the belief that they were spying for the French. And despite the fact that they were eventually dismissed as harmless, Mrs St Albyn remained uneasy about her tenants and ignoring the pleadings of their friend Tom Poole, gave the Wordsworths three months' notice to quit.

Together with Coleridge, the Wordsworths set off for Germany in September 1798, never again to reside in Somerset. Dorothy was destined to continue her journals between 1800 and 1803, from her Lake District home at Grasmere.

Recommended Reading

Journals of Dorothy Wordsworth, OUP, 1971.

Coleridge and Wordsworth. The Crucible of Friendship, Tom Mayberry, Sutton, 1992.

Nearby Strolls

The Cottager Poet: Samuel Taylor Coleridge at Nether Stowey (page 131)

The Schoolgirl Diarist: Anne Garnett at Stogumber (page 135)

32. The Cottager Poet

Samuel Taylor Coleridge at Nether Stowey

Distance: 2 miles (plus optional short stroll to and from Coleridge's Cottage)

Location: Nether Stowey. The village lies off the A39, 8 miles west of Bridgwater.

Park and Start: Library and Visitor Centre car park, Castle Street.

Maps: OS Landranger 181. OS Explorer 140. Grid ref. 190397

Terrain: Along streets, lanes, tracks and fieldpaths. The last two may be muddy after rain. Some steepish gradients.

Refreshments: Choice of inns in the village

Route

1. On leaving the car park, turn right and climb Castle Street, which eventually narrows. Pass Butcher's Lane on the right (return route) and continue to the summit of the road.

2. To see the castle site and the view it offers, turn off right over a stile at this point.

3. To resume the stroll, continue as far as a T-junction. Turn left here and in about 130 metres, turn right to follow a public bridleway sign (Watery Lane).

4. This delightful lane eventually follows the course of a stream. Beyond two stiles, it reaches a crossways of tracks by a cottage.

5. Turn right here up a lane, which dips beyond a right-hand bend at which there are wide views over the gate on the left. From this point, the lane continues to meet a surfaced road, Hack Lane.

6. Turn right. In about 400 metres, and immediately beyond a field gate set back from the road on the left, turn left over a stile (public footpath sign).

7. Follow a fence at first in the direction of the Castle mound. When the fence ends, descend the field to reach a stile about 30 metres to the right of a 30 mph sign visible at the road junction, below.

8. From the stile descend a bank to the road and turn left.

9.   On reaching the junction, bear right along Butcher's Lane and follow it to join the outward route.

10.   Turn left and retrace steps to the start.

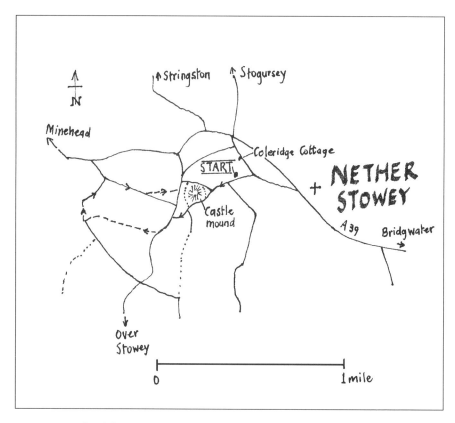

To see Coleridge's Cottage (National Trust)

Continue down Castle Street, passing Poole's House, home of Coleridge's friend Tom Poole, on the left. On reaching the Clock Tower, turn left along Lime Street. Coleridge's Cottage, greatly enlarged and improved since his tenancy from 1796-1798, is 200 metres along on the left (No 35). Opening Times: April to September – Tue, Wed, Thurs, Sun 2-5 p.m.

Literary Connections

It was through his friendship with Tom Poole, a prosperous, self-educated tanner, that Samuel Taylor Coleridge came with Sara, his wife, and baby son David Hartley, to live in a cottage at Nether Stowey during the winter of 1796.

Known then as Gilbard's, the small thatched cottage stood on the Bridgwater-Watchet turnpike. The rent was a mere £7 a year. Poole had provided a gate for his friend into his own spacious garden adjoining, and for a time at least, the poet seemed to have gained the rural idyll he craved.

Then aged twenty-four, Coleridge had already published one book of poems. Now, his career as a poet was firmly established, thanks in no small

Coleridge's Cottage, Nether Stowey

degree to the arrival nearby in the following year of William and Dorothy Wordsworth. Mutual admiration shared between the two poets led to the publication in 1798 of the *Lyrical Ballads*, a joint venture which marked a cornerstone in the development of English poetry. Coleridge's contribution including *Frost at Midnight, The Foster Mother's Tale* and *The Rhyme of the Ancient Mariner*.

Coleridge had always been an enthusiastic walker. Now, however, his passion for the outdoor life intensified, for not only had he the Quantocks and the nearby coastline to explore but he also had stimulating companions – the Wordsworths, Charles Lamb and William Hazlitt – with whom to share the empty and gloriously beautiful hills.

Many of these explorations continued through the winter months and extended into the evenings and after nightfall. This activity led to suspicions among the local people that the newcomers were engaged in spying, this being the time when following the French Revolution, the authorities were quick to investigate such rumours, however ill-founded. There was an element of farce in this; a government investigator was informed that the poets had been overheard in an inn discussing someone called 'Spy Noza', whereas in fact the conversation concerned the philosopher Spinoza.

Although the poets came eventually to be regarded by the authorities as harmless cranks, by 1798, Coleridge's Quantock days were numbered. Together with the Wordsworths, he set sail for Germany in the September of that year. And although he was later to describe his cottage at Nether Stowey as 'miserable' and 'the hovel', he cherished fond memories of his Quantock days: 'The little toe of Quantock,' he wrote, 'is better than the head and shoulders of Surrey and Middlesex.'

Recommended Reading

Coleridge. Early Visions, Richard Holmes, Hodder and Stoughton and Penguin books

Coleridge and Wordsworth. The Crucible of Friendship, Tom Mayberry, Sutton, 1992.

Nearby Strolls

A Quantock Year: The Wordsworths at Alfoxton Park (page 127)

The Schoolgirl Diarist: Anne Garnett at Stogumber (page 135)

33. The Schoolgirl Diarist
Anne Garnett at Stogumber

Distance: 3½ miles

Location: Stogumber. The village lies to the west of the A358, 3 miles SE of Williton.

Park and Start: Limited parking by the church, from which the stroll begins

Maps: OS Landranger 181. OS Outdoor Leisure and Explorer 140. Grid ref. 098373

Terrain: Chiefly along quiet lanes, interspersed with stretches of field path walking. Gradients moderate.

Refreshments: White Horse Inn

Route

1. Facing the church, turn right, pass the post office and walk down to a T-junction.

2. Turn right and follow the road for about a quarter of a mile to reach a lane on the right, with Lane End Cottage commanding the junction.

3. Follow the lane, which climbs steadily and eventually swings to the right before meandering down to a junction.

4. Turn left (Kingswood signpost). Entering the hamlet, keep to the left at a fork (Culverhays signpost). On the left can soon be seen a restored well and pump, with a Luccombe oak planted opposite – Kingswood's millennium project.

5. The lane eventually swings to the right and crosses the Doniford stream before passing beneath a railway bridge (Yard Bridge).

6. Immediately beyond the bend at the bridge, climb steps on the right and go through a kissing gate. Keep a hedge on the right to pass through two field gates. Beyond these, keep a hedge on the left to reach a lane via two handgates.

7. Turn right. Pass a lane on the left and continue to reach a junction. Turn right here (Stogumber signpost) to descend a sunken lane flanked by mossy rocks. Beyond a bridge, the lane climbs steadily before levelling out and joining another lane at a T-junction.

8. Turn right here. Brewers Water Farm, at which Anne Garnett commenced her diary in 1925, is passed on the right.

9. Pass under the railway bridge at Stogumber station and continue over a staggered crossroads towards the village. In about half a mile, turn right along a no-through-road immediately before a road signposted to Vexford on the left. When the road veers to the left, continue straight on along a public footpath between a house and a hedge to reach a crossways of paths through a gate.

10. Turn left. Keep the boundary on the left and pass through two field gates, followed by a kissing gate. On reaching a road, turn left back to the start.

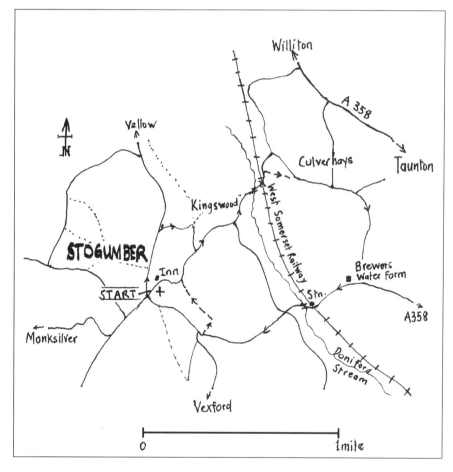

Stogumber

Literary Connection

Between April 1925 and Christmas 1926, a teenage girl, sent down from London to the Somerset countryside on medical advice, kept a diary. This remained unknown outside her family for 60 years until 1986, when the section covering the period April 1925 to May 1926 was published, illustrated by the diarist's own appealing drawings and water colours. Three years later, shortly after her death, the second section also appeared, thus providing the modern reader with a delightfully fresh and intimate insight into Somerset rural life during the inter-war years, as seen through the eyes of a lively, observant schoolgirl.

Born into a literary family, the youthful Anne Garnett was at a distinct advantage when it came to recording her impressions in readable form. And although many pages are devoted to riding, hunting and the social life emanating from these activities, the diarist displays a rare talent in evoking the atmosphere of the period and in describing the range of characters she encountered on her rides, walks and train journeys.

Without doubt, the most memorable of those so described is the diarist's governess, the formidable J.V.S. This lady, daughter of a former local rector, manages to find fault with a succession of farmhouses and cottages at which the couple lodge, thus necessitating numerous moves, all within the Stogumber area. Anne's resilience is such, however, that she takes all this in her stride and despite frequent clashes with her governess, a strong bond of affection between the pair remains.

For many readers, the abiding joys of Anne Garnett's diaries are the entries describing the seasonal changes in the rural scene. Here, artist and writer combine to convey the beauty of the Quantocks, the Brendons and Exmoor, as registered by an avidly impressionable young observer. It comes as no surprise to learn that although she left Somerset to enter art school in the Home Counties and to resume her London family life, Anne's exile was but temporary; in 1930 she married a Somerset solicitor and lived happily in the county for the remainder of her life.

Recommended Reading

Caught from Time, Anne Garnett, Tabb House, 1986.

Fields of Young Corn, Anne Garnett, Tabb House, 1989.

Nearby Strolls

A Quantock Year: The Wordsworths at Alfoxton Park (page 127)

The Cottager Poet: Samuel Taylor Coleridge at Nether Stowey (page 131)

34. A Quantock Honeymoon
Laurence Whistler at Aisholt

Distance: 2¾ miles

Location: Aisholt. The village lies midway between the A39 at Nether Stowey and the A358 at Bishops Lydeard.

Park and Start: The large lay-by at Lawyer's Hill, on the south bank of Hawkridge Reservoir, between Aisholt and Spaxton

Maps: OS Landranger 181. OS Explorer 140. Grid ref. 207360

Terrain: Chiefly along minor roads, tracks and field paths, which may be muddy after rain. Two steepish climbs.

Refreshments: Rising Sun inn, West Bagborough (3 miles SW)

Route

1. Facing the reservoir, turn left and walk along the pavement to a T-junction.

2. Turn right and follow the road as it swings to the left and climbs (Beware traffic – no pavement).

3. At the top of the slope, turn left (Aisholt signpost) and follow the lane. Pass two lanes branching off to the right.

4. On reaching a signpost to Aisholt on the left, keep straight on along a lane signposted to Durborough Farm (no-through-road).

5. In about 250 metres, and 50 metres or so before reaching a lane branching off to the right, follow a signposted footpath through a kissing gate in the hedge on the left.

6. Descend a field to a handgate and down another field to cross a footbridge.

7. Now follow the line indicated by the waymark up the next field to reach Aisholt, opposite the church. (This delightful little church, described by Sir Henry Newbolt as 'so quiet and so eternal', is well worth visiting).

8. The route continues downhill from the church. At the foot, alongside a stream, stands the picturesque thatched Old School House,

once belonging to Sir Henry Newbolt and in which Laurence Whistler and Jill Furse spent their honeymoon.

9. Turn right along the bridleway by the house. This skirts a nature reserve before crossing a ford to reach a fork.

10. Take the right-hand (i.e. lower) path. Continue through a gate and descend to a surfaced lane. Turn left here to reach the road walked earlier.

11. Turn right and retrace the outward route back to the lay-by.

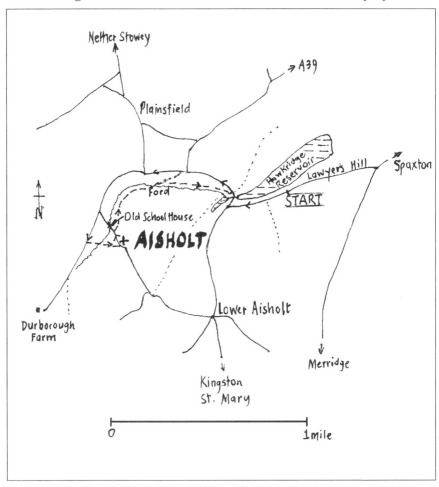

The Old School House, Aisholt

Literary Connection

The fact that this particular literary connection is not only slight but short – a mere six days – is offset by the part it played in what must surely be one of the most poignant love stories of the 20th century – the courtship and tragically short marriage of the engraver and poet Laurence Whistler and the actress Jill Furse.

It was in the twilight of a day in September 1939, barely a week after the outbreak of the Second World War, that the newly weds arrived in a borrowed car at the Old School House at Aisholt, nestling under its thatch in a hollow below the church. The cottage had been lent by the bride's grandmother, Lady Margaret Newbolt, widow of the poet Sir Henry Newbolt (see A Patriot and a Park page 103) who had died the previous year. In his description of this brief interlude in their lives in *The Initials in the Heart,* Laurence Whistler gives a memorable account of blissful days spent exploring remote little churches, picnicking in the Quantock heather and browsing in antique shops.

The couple had first met in the neighbouring county of Wiltshire and a literary connection of sorts had brought them together. Two years earlier, at the suggestion of his artist brother Rex, Laurence Whistler had sent a copy of his book of poems, *The Emperor Heart* to Rex's friend,

Edith Olivier, the novelist, at her home, the Daye House at Wilton. It so happened that Jill Furse was convalescing there at the time and her hostess, on reading the poems to her, noted her favourable response and decided to introduce the couple.

This she did, and on St Valentine's Day 1937 began a love affair, the outcome of which was their marriage in Salisbury Cathedral. The ceremony was conducted by the bride's great-uncle, the Bishop of St Albans, and was followed by the idyllic honeymoon at Aisholt. In the telling of the story of the marriage, the critic Lord David Cecil declared that Laurence Whistler had written "One of the most sustainedly beautiful (prose) poems I have read for a long time."

Recommended Reading

The Initials in the Heart, Laurence Whistler, John Murray, 1964.

To Celebrate Her Living (verse), Laurence Whistler, John Murray, 1967.

Nearby Stroll

In Pursuit of Spring: Edward Thomas at West Bagborough (page 143)

35. In Pursuit of Spring

Edward Thomas at West Bagborough

Distance: 2¼ miles

Location: West Bagborough. The village lies 2 miles east of the A358 near Seven Ash and is 8 miles NW of Taunton.

Park and Start: Lydeard Hill car park, 1 mile east of the village

Maps: OS Landranger 181. OS Explorer 140. Grid ref. 181338

Terrain: Minor roads and bridleways. Mud possible after rain. Steepish gradients.

Refreshments: Rising Sun Inn

Route

1. From the car park, walk down the lane to a three-way junction (Birches Corner).

2. Turn right (West Bagborough signpost). Expansive views are now revealed to the south over Tilbury Park. Pass Tilbury Farm on the right and continue down into the village to reach the Rising Sun Inn.

3. Immediately beyond the inn, turn right up a track, surfaced at first. Go through a gate and follow the lane. There is a good view of Bagborough House and church below to the left.

4. At the top of the lane is a junction of several tracks and paths.

5. Turn right here. In a short distance, go through a gate to the right of a stile and follow the clear track back to the car park.

Literary Connection

In March 1913, the author, essayist and critic Edward Thomas set off from Wandsworth Common in London, where he had spent his youth, on a cycle ride to the Quantock Hills, with the intention of writing a book about the journey.

The 240-mile ride, accomplished in eight days, was, as the book's title *In Pursuit of Spring* suggests, undertaken at that time of year to enable Thomas, with his observant eye and fluent pen, to record a personal impression of the arrival of spring in the West Country.

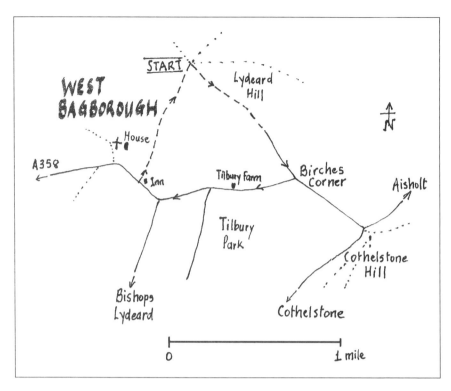

Along a route which took him through Surrey, Hampshire, Wiltshire and Somerset – all counties of which he had an intimate knowledge – Thomas must have filled his notebook with observations of every conceivable kind, for the resulting book ranges freely, with idiosyncratic, yet sharply drawn descriptions of the countryside, towns and villages, people encountered along the way, wildlife – in fact anything that took his fancy. There are too, numerous literary diversions as well as entertaining forays into the realms of place and surname derivations, the prices of various foodstuffs, and fashions in waterproofs and clay pipes.

Reaching West Bagborough, Thomas observed that 'The village houses either touch the edge of the road, or where it is very steep, lie back behind walls which were hanging their white and purple clouds of alyssum and aubretia down to the wayside water.' Entering the inn, he overheard two old men – 'Bent, grinning…using rustic, deliberate, grave speech.' One declared that he had never gardened on a Good Friday, having as a lad known a woman who did so and who died soon afterwards in great pain.

The church and house, West Bagborough

In Pursuit of Spring is notable in being the last of Thomas's country books. By the time of its publication in the following spring, 1914, he had embarked on a friendship with the American poet Robert Frost, which was to have a profound influence on his work. Frost persuaded Thomas that his true vocation lay in poetry, and in the last four years of his life, before his death in battle at Arras in 1917, Edward Thomas emerged as one of the finest and best-loved poets of the 20th century.

To return to *In Pursuit of Spring*. Thomas's ride ended on the north side of Cothelstone Hill, high on the Quantocks, where on the 28 March 1913, he sat in the spring sunshine, content with his achievement: 'I had found Winter's grave; I had found Spring, and I was confident that I could ride home again and find Spring all along the road.'

Note: Edward Thomas also features in a stroll in the Wiltshire section. See: A Soldier's Last Goodbye (page 74)

Recommended Reading

In Pursuit of Spring, Edward Thomas, Nelson, 1914.

Nearby Stroll

A Quantock Honeymoon: Laurence Whistler at Aisholt (page 139)

36. The Restless Rector

Sydney Smith at Combe Florey

Distance: 3½ miles (short option: 1¼ miles)

Location: Combe Florey. The village lies off the A358, 7 miles NW of Taunton.

Park and Start: In the village street near the church, from which the stroll begins.

Maps: OS Landranger 181. OS Explorer 140. Grid ref. 151312

Terrain: Along lanes and field paths, which may be muddy after rain. A few gentle gradients. One very short stretch along the verge of a 'B' road.

Refreshments: The Farmers Arms (off A358, half a mile north)

Route

1. From the church, walk towards the A358, passing the gatehouse on the left and the village hall on the right, to reach a narrow surfaced lane on the left immediately before a cattle shed.

2. Follow this lane. Keep left at a fork by a cottage to cross a stile alongside a gate. Cross a stream and follow its course along a wooded valley.

3. Go through the left-hand of two gates and cross a field to climb a bank. Cross a stile to reach a lane. (A well-preserved lime kiln can be seen a short distance to the right).

4. To continue the stroll, turn left and follow the lane to a junction.

5. To complete the short stroll, turn left at this point back to the start.

6. The route of the longer stroll turns right here. A gentle climb leads to the junction with the B3224.

7. Turn left along the verge for about 200 metres, as far as a lane (no signpost) dipping between trees on the right.

8. A short way down this lane, turn left along a waymarked public footpath.

9. Follow this (a rough track) for about three-quarters of a mile. The track skirts woodland at first, with fine views to the south-west, before continuing through Ash Wood.

10. The route leaves the wood at a fork, climbing gently past a marker post to enter a large field.

11. Cross, keeping a hedge about 100 metres on the right, to reach a lane through a gate.

12. Turn left and follow the lane for almost a mile back to Combe Florey, crossing the B3224 and passing the former home of the Rev. Sydney Smith, the Old Rectory, which is hidden behind a high creeper-clad wall on the left at the approach to the village.

13. On reaching a junction by the former school, turn right back to the start.

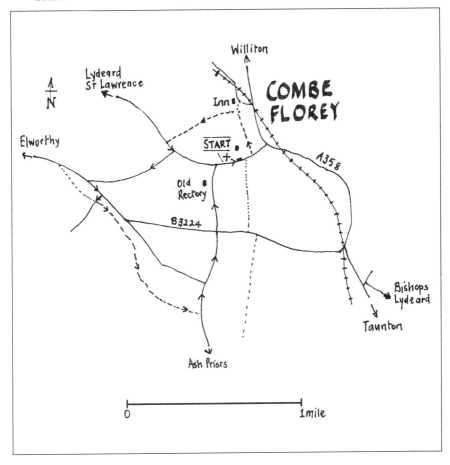

Literary Connections

Despite the ordinariness of his name, the Rev Sydney Smith turned out to be anything but an ordinary village rector, as the people of Combe Florey soon discovered on his arrival there in 1829.

Scholar, wit, author, and co-founder of the *Edinburgh Review*, the new rector was a wealthy man with a wide circle of friends and soon the dilapidated Queen Anne rectory had been restored and the grounds returned to good order. How the villagers must have gaped in wonder as a constant flow of visitors came and went, adding to the whirl of activity generated by the rector's numerous grandchildren. Strange stories soon began to emerge about the new rector's sense of fun; how, in response to a lady guest's lament at the absence of deer in the grounds, he fixed antlers to the heads of his donkeys, and how he tied oranges to his laurel bushes to fool dinner guests on their evening strolls.

There was, however, another side to the Rev Smith's character that was to endear him to his village flock. Outspoken and utterly fearless, he proved to be a true friend of the poor, showing his concern in practical ways. Seeing his duty as attending to the body as well as the soul, he dosed sick children with castor-oil, promoted education and championed the cause of any illiterate parishioner who fell foul of authority.

Combe Florey church

At heart however, this ageing scholar found village life exasperatingly dull. His neighbours, he once wrote, 'look very much like other people's neighbours; their remarks are generally of a meteorological nature'. Though surrounded by books and never for long deprived of stimulating company, he referred to the country as 'a kind of healthy grave' and wrote that 'flowers, green turf, birds, are not worth an hour of rational conversation'.

Even as his life neared its close, his observation that 'I am afraid this country does look enchantingly beautiful', reveals that he conceded only grudgingly that the countryside held any pleasure for him. On his death, aged 74, in 1845, a memorial window was placed in the church.

Combe Florey has other literary connections. From 1956 until his death ten years later, Combe Florey House, with its gatehouse of 1593, was the home of the novelist Evelyn Waugh, and later of his son, Auberon. Until 1924, the Old Manor House belonged for a time to the Rattigan family, a member of which, Terence, was to become a distinguished playwright.

Nearby Stroll

In Pursuit of Spring: Edward Thomas at West Bagborough (page 143)

Exmoor Area

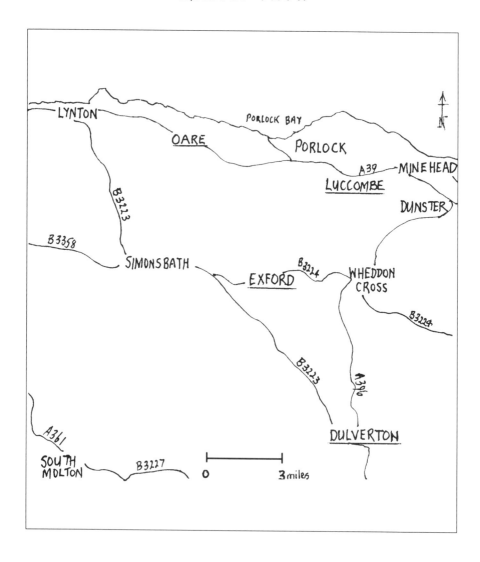

37. The Victorian Romantic

R.D. Blackmore at Oare

Distance: 3¼ miles

Location: Oare lies off the A39 between Porlock and Lynton

Park and Start: Malmsmead National Park car park, a mile west of Oare church

Maps: OS Landranger 180 and 181. OS Outdoor Leisure 9. Grid ref. 791478

Terrain: A mixture of surfaced tracks and footpaths, with short stretches of road walking. Only one steepish gradient.

Refreshments: Malmsmead and Cloud Farm

Route

1. From the main car park at Malmsmead, turn left and left again past Lorna Doone Farm (possible setting for Nicholas Snowe's farm in Blackmore's novel).

2. Cross the packhorse bridge, noticing the ford alongside, and follow the road the short distance to the drive to Cloud Farm on the right (public footpath).

3. On reaching the farm, descend to cross the footbridge and follow the stream (Badgworthy Water). The R.D. Blackmore memorial stone, placed by the path on the centenary of the publication of *Lorna Doone*, is soon reached. The path may be followed beyond this point to see other features relating to the novel. (See OS map).

4. Back at Cloud Farm, the route continues along the footpath sign-posted to Oare Church. This path passes through an open-ended barn and climbs as a track up to a gate. Magnificent views are now revealed way to the west.

5. Beyond, the route follows a grassy path and passes through another gate. Keep a wall on the left over the next field before swinging to the right and climbing a rough track for about 60 metres to go through a gate on the left.

6. The path now descends along the wood side, swinging left with it down to a gate. Beyond this, follow the waymarks downhill to reach a road at Oare, by the church.

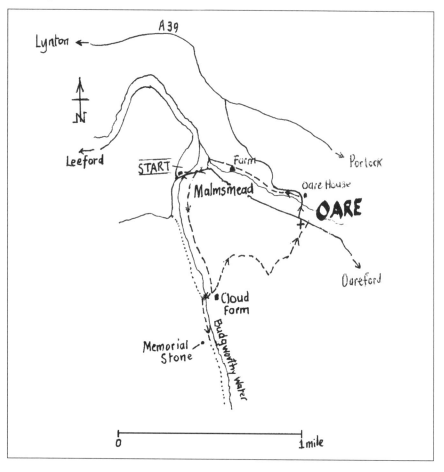

7. Turn left, pass the church, and follow the Porlock signpost at a junction. Cross the bridge spanning Oare Water. Oare House, standing back from the road on the right, is said to have been built from the remains of an ancient farmhouse, linked by some with Plover's Barrows Farm, home of John Ridd.

8. Opposite the drive to Oare House, follow the Malmsmead bridleway sign through a gate. Pass through a wood and follow the gated track towards Parsonage Farm. This is passed on the left to reach a gate.

9. Turn left here, following the Malmsmead sign. Cross a footbridge and climb to a gate by a farm to reach a road.

10. Turn right and follow the road back to the start.

Packhorse bridge, Malmsmead

Literary Connection

It is rare to find an expanse of countryside named on an Ordnance Survey map after a work of fiction. Yet the words Doone Country, printed in bold letters on the Somerset-Devon borderland south of Oare, indicate just that, for they owe their presence solely to a Victorian novel possessing only a tenuous link with reality.

Richard Doddridge Blackmore was in his mid-forties and living near London when one of his early works, *Lorna Doone*, was published in 1869. In all, he wrote fourteen other novels, most of which have long since disappeared without trace; *Lorna Doone*, however, captured the public imagination to such an extent that the corner of Exmoor in which it is set will be known for ever as Doone Country.

Although born near Oxford, Blackmore spent much of his childhood on Exmoor, staying with his grandfather, who was rector of a Devonshire parish. Here, and later, as a pupil at Blundell's School at Tiverton, he heard stories of 'the savage deeds of the outlaw Doones in the depth of Badgworthy Forest', And it was the memory of these tales that provided him with the idea for his novel.

Little did Blackmore realise that the book would cause guide book authors to seek in vain the precise locations of the landscape features he described. Faced with their complaints, a contrite Blackmore admitted that he had allowed himself considerable licence over such detail: 'If I had dreamed that it would ever be more than a book of the moment, the descriptions of scenery – which I know as well as I know my garden – would have been kept nearer to their fact.' Set in the 17th century, the novel was peopled with characters (like his hero John Ridd, Nicholas Snowe and Tom Faggus) – all named after men who lived at that time.

Generations of curious travellers (how many, one wonders, have read the book?) visit Doone country, stand solemnly before the altar in Oare church, contemplating the shooting of fair Lorna in her wedding dress by Carver Doone, and linger around Lorna Doone Farm. As the stroll description reveals, there are several other Doone associations awaiting discovery close by, to say nothing of the pleasure to be had in the scenic delights of this corner of wild Exmoor, in which R.D. Blackmore set his remarkable tale of kidnapping, murder, mystery and triumphant love.

Recommended Reading

Lorna Doone, R.D. Blackmore, Numerous editions.

For a précis of the novel, together with a longer walk, see *A Doone Country Walk,* obtainable from The Exmoor National Park Visitor Centre, Dulverton.

38. *Birdman of Exmoor*
E.W. Hendy at Luccombe

Distance: 3 miles

Location: Luccombe. The village lies off the A39, 3 miles SE of Porlock.

Park and Start: Small car park (with toilets) by phone box in the village

Maps: OS Landranger 181. OS Outdoor Leisure 9. Grid ref. 912445

Terrain: A mixture of minor roads, tracks and field paths, which may be muddy after rain. One short steep climb.

Refreshments: Tea gardens at Horner (1½ miles NW)

Route

1. From the car park, walk up the village street and turn right along the no-through-road by the churchyard lychgate. When the churchyard wall ends, go through a kissing gate on the right, signposted to Chapel Steep.

2. The footpath weaves its way between hedges to reach a road via another kissing gate. Turn left and climb the road to reach a cross-roads (Chapel Cross).

3. Turn left and immediately left again along a bridleway signposted to Brockwell and Wootton Courtenay. Good views of Luccombe, with its wooded backdrop, can be had to the left, while the woodland on the right provides scope for bird watching, especially tits and goldcrests.

4. On reaching a crossways of tracks, continue along the one sign-posted to Brockwell. This clear wide track skirts woodland at first before plunging among the trees.

5. As the track emerges from the wood at a right-hand bend, a good view of Selworthy's white church is revealed in woodland away to the left.

6. Continue down through woodland as far as a path on the left, sign-posted to Holt Ball, reached just before a gate. This path passes through a gate and into more woodland. It then crosses a stream before climbing steeply to reach Holt Ball farm.

7. Pass between the farm buildings and along the lane to reach a road. Turn right and continue as far as a junction.

8. Turn left (signposted to Holt and Blackford). Just beyond a bend, go through a field gate on the left to follow a bridleway signposted to Luccombe Mill.

9. The route passes through an old quarry before swinging first to the left, then to the right and over a field to enter woodland through a gate.

10. On emerging at a lane, turn right along it back to Luccombe and the start.

Note: An informative village trail leaflet can be obtained in the church.

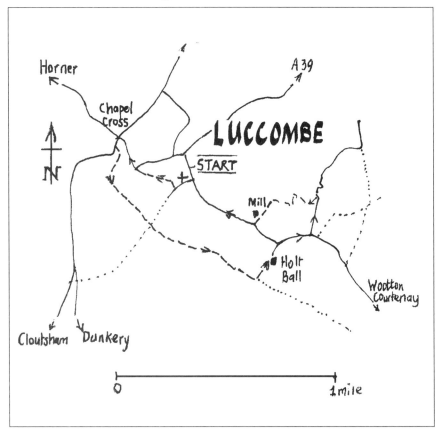

Literary Connection

In 1923, a Cheshire solicitor gave up his practice and moved to Somerset to fulfil a long-cherished ambition. Ernest Hendy (known throughout his literary career by his initials E.W.) was in fact a Wiltshireman, born in Trowbridge, whose professional career had taken him to Manchester. During his west country schooldays however, he had got to know Exmoor and for several years visited the region on holiday, eventually bringing his bride on their honeymoon at the close of the first world war.

Hendy had for many years previously devoted his leisure hours to bird-watching and had corresponded with, among other leading ornithologists, T.A. Coward and W.H. Hudson. Now aged 50, he and his wife had a house built at Porlock and Hendy determined to earn a living through writing about the Exmoor landscape and especially its birds.

Within a year, his one and only book of verse, *Selworthy and Other Poems*, had been published, to be followed by a number of books on birds, including *The Lure of Birdwatching*, *Somerset Birds and Some Other Folk*, *Here and There with Birds* and *More about Birds*. This was to be his last book, published shortly before his death in 1950. However, it is for his general study of his adopted region, *Wild Exmoor throughout the Year*, that Hendy is best known and for which, in the opinion

Luccombe

of one authority, 'he is by far the best and truest interpreter of wild Exmoor.'

Although Hendy's knowledge and love of Exmoor extended over the entire region, he was especially fond of the village of Luccombe, as a memorial tablet on the church wall recalls.

Like Coward and Hudson – 'my apostles, my guides, philosophers and friends in bird matters' – E.W. Hendy was a devoted protectionist and his views on egg-collecting, once a mania with some ornithologists, were so uncompromising that he resigned from one learned body in protest against the activities of some of its members.

Hendy was not only a first-rate ornithologist but a writer of beautiful prose, as this brief description of Horner Water reveals: 'where pleached boughs arch its course, dippers plunge and tumble on stickles chequered by sunlight, or bob their snowy gorgets upon mossy boulders.'

Recommended Reading

Wild Exmoor throughout the Year, E.W. Hendy, 1930, Reprinted 1947.

More about Birds, E.W. Hendy, Country Life, 1950.

39. An Exmoor Explorer
W.H. Hudson at Exford

Distance: 2½ miles

Location: Exford. The village lies on the B3224, 10 miles SE of Minehead.

Park and Start: The village car park, down the lane opposite the Crown Hotel

Maps: OS Landranger 181. OS Outdoor Leisure 9. Grid ref. 855383

Terrain: Entirely along tracks and footpaths, sections of which may be muddy after rain. Gentle gradients.

Refreshments: Choice of inns in Exford

Route

1. From the car park, continue out of the village and through a kissing gate to follow a field path with the River Exe on the right.

2. A second kissing gate gives access to the river bank. Beyond two more gates, by Court Farm, follow the sign Lover's Lane, Highercombe and Lyncombe.

3. Ignore a path to the church on the left. Instead, keep straight on to cross a stile by a farm building. The path divides here. Follow the Highercombe sign, keeping a hedge bank on the left.

4. Cross a stile and keep to the same line over the next field. In the 3rd field, cross half right to a gate in a fence, leading down through a wood.

5. Cross a stream over a plank bridge and climb towards a T-junction of paths at Highercombe Farm, reached through a handgate.

6. Turn right here and follow the gated track downhill. At the foot of the slope, just before the gate leading to Lyncombe Farm, turn right over a stile.

7. The path sweeps in an arc over low-lying ground to reach the bank of the Exe over a stile. Cross two more stiles and take a well-worn path with gorse bushes on the left.

8. At the field end, go through a gateway and keep a fence on the right to reach a stile. The path now climbs to join the outward route by the farm building passed earlier.

9. Retrace steps to the start.

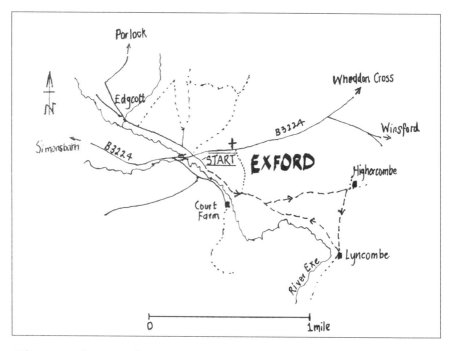

Literary Connection

Like that other great naturalist, Richard Jefferies, the author W.H. Hudson delighted in his discovery of Exmoor. Like Jefferies too, he was especially drawn to a river – in this case the Exe – and in a chapter entitled *Following a River* in his book *Afoot in England*, published in 1909, he describes how he traced this 'beautiful silvery serpent that was my friend and companion', not merely on a whim, but because his forefathers had dwelt for generations beside it, thus bestowing upon it an almost sacred appeal.

Attempting to follow a river, Hudson soon discovered, was fraught with difficulties. Closed-off footpaths, overgrown hedges, barbed wire – 'man's devilish improvement on the bramble' – impeded his progress in places, while encounters with gamekeepers and suspicious landowners presented further tests of his resolve. Even walking the riverside roads was not entirely free from hazards; Edwardian motorists, Hudson wrote in exasperation, 'cover and blind us and choke us with dust and insolently hoot-hoot at us.'

Nevertheless, he pressed doggedly on, determined to achieve a long-cherished ambition to follow the Exe from its source beyond

Exford

Simonsbath down through Devon to Exeter and Exmouth. On looking back at this eventful journey however, it was of the village of Exford that he retained the fondest memories. 'The village is not picturesque,' he conceded, 'Its one perennial charm is the swift river that flows through it, making music on its wide sandy and pebbly floor.'

As a naturalist, noted for his knowledge and love of birds, Hudson found the Exe at Exford especially alluring on account of the wagtails. Both the pied and the grey were present, 'finding little half-uncovered stones in the current to perch upon.' The delicately-coloured grey wagtail's habit of flicking its exceptionally long tail he likened to the flirtatious way a Spanish señora used her fan – its tail serving as an ornament and as a means of expressing emotion.

Watching the flitting wagtails, Hudson noticed a shabbily dressed little girl wade out into the shallows, to stand laughing at her own reflection in the rippling wavelets: 'Like the wagtails, she looked in harmony with her surroundings.'

Recommended Reading

Afoot in England, W.H. Hudson, Dent. Several editions

Note: W.H. Hudson also features in a stroll in the Wiltshire section. See A Wanderer in Wiltshire (page 70)

40. The Naturalist's Summer
Richard Jefferies at Dulverton

Distance: 3 miles

Location: Dulverton. The town lies off the A396, approximately midway between Minehead and Tiverton.

Park and Start: Park in one of the town car parks. The stroll commences from the bridge over the River Barle at the western extremity of the town.

Maps: OS Landranger 181. OS Outdoor Leisure 9. Grid ref. 912278

Terrain: Apart from short stretches of pavement walking at the beginning and end of the stroll, the route follows clear, well-surfaced paths and roads used as public paths. Several steepish gradients.

Refreshments: Choice of inns and restaurants in the town

Route

1. Cross the bridge over the River Barle and turn right immediately along a lane.

2. The lane soon climbs as far as a private drive, beyond which it continues as a footpath along a sunken lane, climbing to the right.

3. On reaching a fork, keep to the right (i.e. straight on) along a path signposted to Tarr Steps and Hawkridge.

4. Level at first, this delightful woodland-edge path eventually passes close to the river before climbing via steps to give impressive views. It then descends and levels out to pass farm buildings and reach a road.

5. Turn right and continue to cross Marsh Bridge. (Notice the old packhorse bridge on the right.)

6. Keep right at a fork and left at a second, a short distance beyond, opposite a road junction, to follow a public path signposted to Court Down and Northcombe.

7. There follows a steady climb up Loose Hall Lane to reach a T-junction of lanes. Turn right here (Dulverton signpost) and follow the lane back to the town, reached down steps at the end of the churchyard wall.

Literary Connection

In June 1882, the Wiltshire-born naturalist and author Richard Jefferies arrived in Somerset from his London home to gather material for his book *Red Deer*. Despite suffering already from the tubercular illness that was to prove fatal five years later, the 34-year-old found Exmoor and the Quantocks very much to his liking and his stay during that memorable summer yielded not only one of his most outstanding books but also three delightful essays.

Jefferies was fortunate in having as his guide during his Exmoor rambles the celebrated huntsman and authority on the red deer, Fred Heal. Although as a naturalist and prose poet his admiration for the deer may well have conflicted somewhat with the sport of hunting, his book provides a dispassionate account of the practices and techniques employed by the hunt. At the same time it is clear that Jefferies thrilled at the sight of the noble beast 'standing in the fern beside a bush with his head down as if feeding. The great oak-woods were about him and the sunlight fell on the golden red of his coat'.

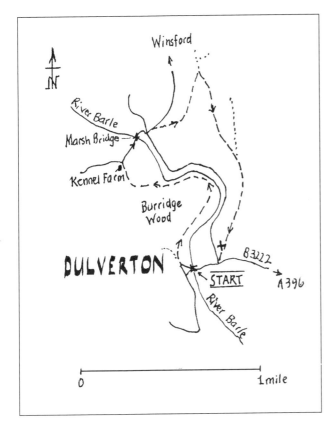

Not content to confine his attention exclusively to the red deer, Jefferies records in beautiful prose his impressions of the Exmoor landscape and in particular of the River Barle. In his essay *Summer in Somerset*, he conveys the subtle changes along the riverside, from 'a

Barle Bridge, Dulverton

wild rush of crowded waters rotating as they go, shrill voices calling' as he wandered upstream, to the more placid reaches downstream, where the overhanging trees and ferns gave rise to a mingling of tints on the water 'washed together by the slow swirl, they produced a shade – the brown of the Barle – lost in darkness where the bank overhangs ... and the river for a while flows in quietness, broad and smooth.'

By contrast to his quiet and reflective wanderings along the Barle, Jefferies found the little town of Dulverton a scene of bustling activity: 'The road is jammed tight between cottages: so narrow is the lane that foot passengers huddle up in doorways to avoid the touch of the wheels.' He arrived just as the farm labourers were heading homewards from their work in the fields, carrying windblown branches from the old oaks to burn on their cottage fires and listened once more to the brown Barle as it rushed through the town in the still evening air.

Recommended Reading

Red Deer, Richard Jefferies, First published 1884

Field and Hedgerow (Essays), Richard Jefferies, First published 1887.

Note: Richard Jefferies also features in a stroll in the Wiltshire section. See The Naturalist at Home (page 19)

Bibliography

These entries are supplementary to the recommended reading on individual strolls.

Wiltshire

Exploring Historic Wiltshire: Vol.1 – North, Ken Watts, Ex Libris Press

Exploring Historic Wiltshire: Vol.2 – South, Ken Watts, Ex Libris Press

The Marlborough Downs, Ken Watts, Ex Libris Press

The Wiltshire Village Book, Michael Marshman, Countryside Books

A History of Wiltshire, Bruce Watkin, Phillimore

Wiltshire, Mark Child, Shire Publications

Moonraker County, Lornie Leete-Hodge, Sutton

Somerset

Somerset: With Bath and Bristol, Shirley Toulson, Pimlico

The Somerset Village Book, Somerset Federation of WIs, Countryside Books

A History of Somerset, Robert Dunning, Phillimore

Somerset and Avon, Robert Dunning, Sutton

Somerset Villages, Robin Bush, Dovecote Press

Exmoor and the Quantocks. John Earle, Cicerone Press

Exmoor: Official National Park Guide, Brian Pearce. David and Charles

Visitor and Tourist Information Centres

Wiltshire

Amesbury: Redworth House, Flower Lane. SP4 7HG. 01980-622833

Avebury: The Great Barn. 01672-539425

Chippenham: The Citadel, Bath Road. 01249-706333

Devizes: Cromwell House, Market Place. 01380-729408

Malmesbury: Town Hall, Market Lane. SN16 9BZ. 01666-823748

Marlborough: George Lane Car Park. 01672-513989

Mere: The Square. BA12 6JJ. 01747-861211

Salisbury: Fish Row. SP1 1EJ. 01722-334956

Trowbridge: St. Stephen's Place. 01225-777054

Warminster: Central Car Park. 01985-218548

Somerset:

Dulverton: Exmoor National Park Visitor Centre, Fore Street. 01398-323841. Written and winter enquiries: Exmoor National Park Authority, Exmoor House, Dulverton. TA22 9HL. 01398-323665

Dunster: Exmoor National Park Visitor Centre, Dunster Steep. 01643-821835

Minehead: 17 Friday Street. 01643-702624

Porlock: Visitor Centre, West End, High Street. 01643-863150

Wells: Town Hall, Market Place. BA5 2RB. 01749-672552

Yeovil: Petter's House, Petter's Way. BA20 1SH. 01935-462991

Index